ANNEMARIE SCHIMMEL

ISLAMIC LITERATURES OF INDIA

A HISTORY
OF INDIAN LITERATURE

EDITED BY JAN GONDA

PART OF VOL. VII

Vol 8(1)

OTTO HARRASSOWITZ · WIESBADEN

ANNEMARIE SCHIMMEL

ISLAMIC LITERATURES OF INDIA

1973
OTTO HARRASSOWITZ · WIESBADEN

A HISTORY OF INDIAN LITERATURE

Contents of Vol. VII/VIII

Gesamtherstellung: Allgäuer Zeitungsverlag GmbH, Kempten
Printed in Germany
ISBN 3 447 01509 8

Annemarie Schimmel

ISLAMIC LITERATURES OF INDIA*

The 'Islamic Literatures of India' comprise almost the whole of Arabic, Persian, and Turkish written in the Subcontinent as well as Urdu, Sindhi, Pashto, Panjabi and in part Bengali literature. But since the various languages of Indian origin will be treated separately, we here confine ourselves to a short survey of the Arabic, Persian and Turkish works produced in Indo-Pakistan.[1] The contribution of the Muslims in India to Islamic learning is very large, and the amount of literature—both poetry and prose—composed in Persian in the Subcontinent is larger than that produced in Iran proper. Therefore, only a bare outline of the most important literary trends can be attempted. Since many scholars and poets used two and sometimes three languages simultaneously, it is impossible to draw distinct boundary-lines.[2]

---

* The transcription of well-known proper names—including Shāh and Khān—follows the generally accepted English usage; only the Oriental titles and less known names are given in scholarly transcription. Not all titles have been translated, since that would prove too repetitious; the most frequently occurring Arabic and Persian expressions used in titles of books are: *ta'rīḫ* (pl. *tawārīḫ*) History, *ṭabaqāt*: Classes (e.g. historical works arranged according to the groups of persons in different times), *ma'āṯir* 'Memorabilia,' *muntaḫab* 'Selection,' *farhang* 'Dictionary,' *rauḍa* (pl. *riyāḍ*) 'Garden, Enclosed Place,' *ruq'āt* 'Scraps, Short notes,' *Dīvān* 'collection of poetical works,' *taḏkira* 'memorial, biographies.'

[1] Abbreviations: GAL: Brockelmann, Geschichte der arabischen Literatur, I—III, and S: Supplement, Leiden since 1937.—E: H. Ethé, Neupersische Literatur, in: Geiger-Kuhn, Grundriß der iranischen Philologie, Straßburg 1903 vol. II.—R: J. Rypka, History of Iranian Literatures, Dordrecht 1968. – ZA: Zubaid Ahmad, India's Contribution to Arabic Literature, Lahore ²1968. – Storey: H. Storey, Persian Literature, A bio-bibliographical Survey, London 1927–53, 1958. – MM: D. N. Marshall, Mughals in India, Bombay 1967 (reference to the numbers). IC: Islamic Culture, Hyderabad. Since these books usually refer to the catalogues of European and Indian libraries we have only in exceptional cases referred to these.

[2] General Surveys: I. H. Qureshi, The Muslim Community of the Indo-Pakistan Subcontinent, 's-Gravenhage 1962; Aziz Ahmad, Studies in Islamic Culture in the Indian Environment, Oxford 1964; The same, An intellectual History of Islam in India, Edinburg 1969 (both books with extensive bibliographies); M. Mujeeb, The Indian Muslims, Montreal–London 1969; Tara Chand, The influence of Islam on Indian Culture, Allahabad 1946; Yusuf Husain, L'Inde Mystique au Moyen Age, Paris 1929; the same, Glimpses of Medieval Indian Culture, London ²1959; S. M. Ikram, Muslim Civilization in India, New York 1964. Numerous studies about Indo-Muslim literature are contained in the useful journal *Indo-Iranica*, published in Calcutta.

The connections of the Subcontinent with the Arabs go back to Sumerian times; trade-relations between Arabia, mainly the Yemen and Hadramaut, and Sind and the Malabar Coast existed in ancient times.[3] First contacts of the Muslims with the Indian Subcontinent were established shortly after the Prophet Muhammad's death (632 AD); under his second successor 'Umar a naval expedition was led against Surat (637); four years later the first invasion of Sind took place. It is said that five companions of the Prophet came to India to introduce the Islamic religion there; they could have acted as transmitters of Prophetic traditions, *ḥadīṯ*.[4] Islamisation proper, however, began in the year 711 when Muhammad ibn al-Qāsim conquered Sind up to Multan and laid the foundations of the Muslim rule which continued till our day.

Later, the relations between Sind and the court of Bagdad became quite close; a number of Sindhi scholars came to the Arab countries, including the great jurist al-Auzā^cī (d. 773) as well as the first author of a *kitāb al-maġāzī* about the Prophet's warfare, Abū Ma^cšar (d. 786). Even some poets from Sind gained fame among the Arabs: Abū 'Aṭā's poetry was considered worthy of being included in the anthology *al-Ḥamāsa* (although the author was not able to recite Arabic correctly, pronouncing—as Sindhis and Gujeratis still do—*š* as *s*, *ǧ* as *z*).[5]—Indian rhetoric was famous enough in Iraq to be discussed by al-Ǧāhiẓ (d. 867) in his *kitāb al-bayān*, and the role of the Muslims of Sind as transmitters of Indian medical, mathematical and astronomical knowledge cannot be overrated.[6] Apparently the study of Prophetic traditions was popular in Sind, insofar as one can judge from the proper names of traditionalists, such as as-Sindī, ad-Daibulī, al-Manṣūrī, etc. The Arab geographers give a lively picture of theological activity in the country: Manṣūra, the capital, was not only a stronghold of the Ḥanafī but also of the Ẓāhirī legal school.[7] We can surmise that mystical currents too had developed in this part of the Muslim world, since the great Sufi saint al-Ḥallāǧ travelled in 905 through Gujrat and Sind up to Kashmir to discuss religious topics with the inhabitants. The conquest of Multan and the adjacent provinces by the Ismailis who came from Bahrain led to a setback in *ḥadīṯ* studies. Little is known about their literary

---

[3] About the early relations between Arabia and the Subcontinent cf. Sayyid Sulayman Nadwi, Literary Relations between Arabia and India, IC 1932–3; the same, Commercial Relations of India with Arabia, IC 1933; the same, Religious Relations between Arabia and India, IC 1934; the same, Muslim Colonies in India before the Muslim Conquest, IC 1934, 1935; Maqbul Ahmad, Indo-Arab Relations, Bombay 1969.

[4] M. Ishaq, India's Contribution to the Study of Hadith Literature, Dacca 1955.

[5] Abu Tammām, al-Ḥamāsa, ed. M. Taufīq, Cairo s.d., Book I Nr. 6. Cf. N. B. Baloch, The Dīwān of Abū 'Aṭā' of Sind, IC 23/1949.

[6] About India as the homeland of *ḥikma*, 'wisdom' cf. Mas'ūdī, murūǧ aḏ-ḏahab I 76, Ibn al-Qifṭī, ta'rīḫ al-ḥukamā', ed. Lippert, p. 266, etc.

[7] H. Gildemeister, Scriptorum Arabum de Rebus indicis loci, Bonn 1838; S. Reinaud, Fragments Arabes et Persans relatifs à l'Inde, Paris 1845; G. Ferrand, Voyage du Merchant Arabe Sulayman en Inde et en Chine 851, Paris 1922.

activities in the Subcontinent in early days;[8] but in later centuries they produced a remarkable number of Arabic writings,[9] and later Ismaili literature in Sindhi, Cachchi and Gujerati is highly interesting from the religious and linguistic view-points.[10]

After Mahmud of Ghazna had conquered Northwestern India the influence of Islam grew everywhere;[11] a thorough study of Arabic was required of every theologian in the *madrasas* (colleges). The interest of the scholars was directed more towards *fiqh*, e.g. the Ḥanafī legal system the knowledge of which was necessary for the career of a judge or any other higher governmental position. Yet, despite the importance of Ḥanafī law only a few original books on this subject were composed in Muslim India in early times.[12]

From the 13th to the 15th centuries, the torchbearers of *ḥadīṯ* studies—and of Islamic thought in general—were mainly the mystics who attempted to follow closely the example of the Prophet and were for this reason interested in collecting as many traditions as possible: the collections by Niẓāmuddīn Auliyā', Bahā'uddīn Zakariya, and, later, Šarafuddīn Manērī are typical of this trend. Slightly earlier, i.e. in the first half of the 13th century, the most important book written on *ḥadīṯ* was the *mašāriq al-anwār*. Composed by al-Ḥasan aṣ-Ṣaġānī al-Lāhōrī, it was destined to become the guidebook of the subsequent generations.[13] aṣ-Ṣaġānī, who was primarily a Ḥanafī scholar, reached Bagdad after long wandering and was sent by the caliph an-Nāṣir to the court of Iltutmish in Delhi in 1218; after twenty years he returned once more to Bagdad where he died in 1252. He popularized the two classical *ḥadīṯ* works, the *ṣaḥīḥān* of al-Buḫārī (d. 875) and of al-Muslim (d. 870), taking from them some 2253 traditions. According to legend, Niẓāmuddīn Auliyā' of Delhi—mystic and preacher[14]—learned the *mašāriq* by heart, as an expiation for having committed to memory in his youth the *maqāmāt al-Ḥarīrī*, that charming rhetorical novel which belonged to the basic books of instruction in Arabic literature in Indian *madrasas*. From ca. 1320 on, more than a thousand commentaries of the *mašāriq* have been written; one of them was composed by Gīsūdarāz, the Čištī saint at the Bahmani court (d. 1422) who translated the whole collection into Persian. Gīsūdarāz also collected an *arbā'īn*, a group of 40 traditions, after the model of an-Nawawī's (d. 1277) *arba'īn*—a book often

---

[8] S. M. Stern, Ismaili Propaganda and Fatimid Rule in Sind, IC 1949.

[9] About Ismaili literature in Arabic between 1533 and 1770 vd. GAL S II 608ff. For the whole complex: W. Ivanow, Guide to Ismaili Literature, London 1933.

[10] G. Khakee, The Dasa Avatara of the Satpanthi Ismailis and the Imam Shahis of Indo-Pakistan, Ph. D. Diss. Harvard, 1972.

[11] al-Bīrūnī, ta'rīḫ al-Hind: Alberuni's India, an account of the religion, philosophy, litterature, chronology, astronomy, customs, laws and astrology of India about 1030, ed. E. Sachau, London 1887, engl. by E. Sachau 1888, ²1910.

[12] Abū Bakr Isḥāq al-Multānī Ibn Tāǧ, ca. 1335: GAL S II 310 (with two more scholars); Storey I 36; ZA I 1, III 4, IV 2.

[13] GAL I 360, S I 613; ZA II 1, IX 1, XI 2.

[14] For his Arabic sermons vd. ZA X 1.

commented upon and imitated in India.[15] His elder contemporary Sayyid Ǧalāl Buḫārī Maḫdūm-i Ǧihāniyān (d. 1382), the Suhrawardi leader of Ucch, continued the work of Bahā'uddīn Zakariya, the saint of Multan, and commented, like Gīsūdarāz, upon the *mašāriq* and Baġawī's *maṣābīḥ as-sunna*, a popular *ḥadīṯ* collection which is still in use among Indo-Pakistani scholars.[16]

An important centre for the activities of traditionalists was East Bengal; Abū Taw'ama al-Buḫārī (d. 1300), a Ḥanbalī scholar, settled in the capital, Sunargaon. Among his disciples one may mention Baranī (d. 1381) from Patna. All his pupils travelled widely in the Muslim world in search of *ḥadīṯ*. The situation was similar in Jawnpur where a school of tradition flourished. In Kashmir, the Sufi leader Sayyid 'Alī Hamaḏānī al-Amīr al-Kabīr[17] who reached the country in 1371 with 700 followers encouraged Islamic studies and composed, in addition to numerous mystical works, a collection of seventy *ḥadīṯ* supporting the special claims of the Prophet's family.

In Southern India, both the Bahmanids in the Deccan (1347–1526) and the rulers of Gujrat encouraged the study of *ḥadīṯ*;[18] scholars from their countries wandered to the Hijaz and Egypt while Arabic specialists came to Gujrat to teach Islamics, among them Badruddīn ad-Damāmīmī.[19] Waǧīhuddīn Guǧrātī (d. 1589) is the most outstanding and prolific scholar of this group.[20] And the Indian scholars of the 15th and 16th centuries could proudly claim to be disciples of the foremost masters of the Islamic world, like Ibn Ḥaǧar al-'Askalānī (d. 1448), as-Saḫāwī (d. 1488), and Zakariya al-Anṣārī (d. 1520). As late as 1600 an Arabic chronicle of the province of Gujrat was composed by 'Alī Muḥammad al-Makkī al-Ulūġḫānī (d. after 1611).[21]

Gujrat was a natural resort for scholars both from foreign countries and from the neighbouring kingdoms. For in Southern India, several rulers professed the Shia creed, thus in Bijapur the 'Adilšahis (only Ibrāhīm I, 1534–57, and Ibrāhīm II, 1580–1627, were Sunnis and had acquired a number of *ḥadīṯ* books for the royal library). Muslims saints were recorded in Bijapur from the 11th century. Later, one of the best scholars of Arabic, Zainuddīn al-Ma'barī al-Malībārī (d. 1522), lived there for a long while.[22] His literary activities embrace nearly every field of Islamic learning; from mysticism and homiletics to *ḥadīṯ* and *fiqh*; he wrote also learned Arabic poetry, thus the Sufi poem *hidāyat al-aḏkiyā*

[15] ZA IV 6.

[16] Ibn al-Farrā' al-Baġawī, d. 1112, GAL I 363, S I 620. — Cf. H. Feldman, Revolution in Pakistan, London 1967, p. VII.

[17] Cf. J. K. Teufel, Eine Lebensbeschreibung des Scheich 'Alī-i Hamaḏānī, Leiden 1962; GAL S II 311; ZA I 2, II 3, IV 4, VI 1; E 349.

[18] S. C. Misra, Muslim Communities in Gujerat, London 1964.

[19] GAL II 26, S II 21; ZA II 4, IX 5.

[20] GAL S II 605; ZA I 9, II 9, III 24, IV 19, V 9; VII 1, IX 17.

[21] ẓafar al-wālih bi-Muẓaffar wa ālihi, An Arabic History of Gujarat, ed. E. D. Ross, I–III, London 1910–1928. GAL S II 599; ZA VII 5; MM 44.

[22] GAL S II 311ff.; ZA IV 9; ZA mentions his son as an Arabic scholar; GAL II 417, SII 604 speaks of his grandson Zainuddīn al-Malībārī as an author on *fiqh*.

'Guidance of the Intelligent' to which his son added a commentary. His grandson, Zainuddīn ibn 'Abdul 'azīz al-Ma'barī (d. 1583), is best known from his Arabic chronicle *tuḥfat al-muǧāhidīn* 'Gift of the Fighters' which deals with the proceedings of the Portuguese at the Malabar coast;[23] his brother, Muhammad ibn 'Abdul 'azīz al-Kalīkūtī, wrote an *urǧūza* in 500 Arabic verses on the same topic, to praise the Raja of Kalikut who, though a Hindu, supported his Muslims subjects against the Portuguese:[24]

fa'inna hāḏī qiṣṣatun 'aǧība
fī šarḥi ḥarbin šānuhu ġarība . . .

"This is a wonderful story, giving account of a strange war occurring in the land of Malabar—and the like of it never took place in that country—between the lover of the Muslims, the Zamorin, and his enemy, the infidel Farangis.
I have versified some part of it, by God, so that all kings may hear the story; so that they may, when they hear it, ponder over the war or may take a lesson, so that the story may go forth in all directions, especially to Syria and Mesopotamia, so that they may know of the courage of the king Zamorin who is well known in all places, the ruler of the celebrated Kalikut—may it ever remain prosperous by the grace of God." (Zubaid Ahmad, p. 244).

The simple poem must have appealed to a large circle of Arabic speaking people in that area. Still later, members of the famous scholarly family of al-'Aidarūs settled in Bijapur and promoted Arabic learning. Among the numerous works of 'Abdulqādir Muḥyī ud-Din al-'Aidarūs (d. ca. 1622), his account of the scholars and Sufis in Gujerat and South Arabia *(an-nūr as-sāfir fī aḫbār al-qarn al-'āšir)* is most valuable.[25] Later, Ǧa'far al-'Aidarūs (d. 1653) translated into Arabic Prince Dārā Shikoh's hagiography *safīnat al-auliyā'*.[26]

In Central India, the *madrasa* at Burhanpur was to develop into one of the centres of Islamic learning during the later 15th and 16th centuries. A mystically inclined scholar from this place, 'Alī al-Muttaqī (1481–1568), compiled a useful collection of *ḥadīṯ*. Having been *qāḍī* in his hometown, he left Burhanpur for Gujrat, and eventually died in Mecca.[27] The leading traditionist of Delhi, 'Abdulḥaqq Dihlawī (d. 1654) has devoted to him and another Indian saint in Mecca his Arabic work *zād al-muttaqīn* 'The nourishment of the Pious.' It may be mentioned at random that a considerable number of Indian scholars

---

[23] GAL S II 599; ZA II 8, III 22, IV 19, VIII 3; the *tuḥfa* was translated into English by Lt. Rowlandson 1833, into Portuguese by D. Lopes 1898, and by Ḥakīm Sayyid Ghulām Allāh Qādiri, Hyderabad 1931.

[24] Cf. ZA p. 243, XI 6.

[25] GAL II 419, S II 617; ZA I 15, IV 26, V 14, VIII 6, X 5; MM 117. About the family al-'Aidarūs cf. F. Wüstenfeld, Die Çufiten in Süd-Arabien im XI (XVII) Jahrhundert, in Abh. der hist.-phil. Klasse der Kgl. Ges. d. Wiss., Göttingen XXX 1, 1883, mainly Nr. 51–79. The article contains most valuable information about the relations of Indian and Arabian scholars.

[26] ZA VIII 12.

[27] GAL II 384, S II 518; ZA I 7, II 6, IV 14; the *kanz al-'ummāl* was printed in Hyderabad/Deccan 1945.

settled in the holy city of Mecca during the 16th and 17th centuries, some of them excelling in Arabic works on Sufism, others translating the classics of the Naqšbandīya order, like Ǧāmī's (d. 1492) *nafaḥāt al-uns* or 'Ali ibn Ḥusain's *rašaḥāt 'ain al-ḥayāt* into Arabic.[28]—As to 'Alī al-Muttaqī, his main interest lay in the work on tradition by the Egyptian polyhistorian and theologian Ǧalāl-uddīn as-Suyūṭī (d. 1505). After may revisions and changes of his original rewording of as-Suyūṭī's *al-ǧāmi' aṣ-ṣaġīr* he produced the *kanz al-'ummāl*, 'The Treasure of the Working,' an encyclopedic collection of *ḥadīṯ* usefully arranged according to subjects which is, still, one of the most widely used works on tradition. 'Alī (being a member of the Qādirī and Šāḏilī orders) also classified the most widely read work of Sufi wisdom, Ibn 'Aṭā'ullāh's (d. 1309) *ḥikam* 'Wise Sayings' along with its commentaries. 'Alī's disciples abridged his work and commented upon it time and again to such an extent that its very name has, in later times, become the symbol for dry scholarship and traditionalism: like the textbook of Ḥanafī law by al-Qudūrī (d. 1037) the *kanz* has often been mentioned in a derogatory sense by the mystical poets of India who relied rather on loving experience than on learned books.

During 'Alī al-Muttaqī's lifetime, the first Indian commentary on Buḫārī's *ṣaḥīḥ* was written by 'Abdulawwal az-Zaidpūrī (d. 1560) who was invited to Akbar's court on behalf of Bairam Khān.[29] Another scholar of this period, Ǧamāluddīn ibn Ṭāhir al-Fatanī from Gujrat (d. 1578), studied in Mecca under Ibn Ḥaǧar al-Haiṯamī; he composed useful works on the correct reading of names which occur in traditions, and a Persian dictionary of difficult words in *ḥadīṯ*. Al-Fatanī was assassinated by followers of the Mahdi of Jawnpur whose theology he had opposed.[30] The production of secondary works, such as super-commentaries and works on vocalizing difficult texts, remained the main occupation of Indian scholars of *ḥadīṯ* during the following centuries. Then, in the 19th and early 20th century, the *ṣaḥīḥ* of Buḫārī has been translated into Urdu and Bengali.

It goes without saying that Indian Muslims commented upon the Quran. 'Alā'uddīn al-Mahā'imī's (d. 1431)[31] *tabṣīr ar-raḥmān* is considered one of the most reliable older Indian commentaries although its author was a follower of Ibn 'Arabī's theosophical mysticism and composed mystical works as well. His contemporary Qadi Šihābuddīn Daulatābādī (d. 1445) excelled not only by writing the first Persian commentary of the Quran in India *(al-baḥr al-mawwāǧ)* in which he treated mainly problems relating to *fiqh* and dogmatics; he won fame as commentator upon Pazdawī's *uṣūl al-fiqh*, a handbook of Ḥanafī law as well. As a grammarian he commented upon Ibn Ḥāǧib's (d. 1249) *kāfiya*, a poem on Arabic syntax; besides this work, the so-called *šarḥ-i Hindī*,

---

[28] Cf. ZA p. 95; also Y. FRIEDMAN, Shaikh Ahmad Sirhindi, Montreal 1971.
[29] ZA II 5, III 19.
[30] GAL S II 601f.; ZA II 7, IX 14; MM 1141.
[31] GAL II 221, S I 310f. ZA p. 15; I 3, III 12, IV 7, V 3.

he composed a book of his own on Arabic grammar, *al-iršād fī'n-naḥw* 'Direction in Grammar' which became the standard work in Indian schools.[32]

Among the commentaries of the Quran composed in the Subcontinent the strangest one is no doubt the *sawāṭi' al-ilhām* 'Brilliant Lights of Inspiration' by Faiḍī, Akbar's court-poet (d. 1595); it consists exclusively of undotted letters.[33] This was, in fact, a major achievement since this form excludes the use of most verbal forms in Arabic. Not surprisingly, its contents are almost lost behind the artificial form.

The high time of Arabic poetry in the Subcontinent coincided with the Mughal period, although its main ground was the Deccan.[34] The rulers of Golconda and the neighbouring Muslim states had never come as much under Persian influence as the provinces in the Northern part of India. The relations of South India with Arabic culture have always been strong as is visible from the large number of Muslim Arab settlements on the south coast. When Ibn Baṭṭūṭa, in the 14th century, visited Hanawar in South India, he found there 23 schools for Muslim boys, 13 for girls; indeed, Ponani at the Malabar coast was one of the great centres of Islamic learning.

It is therefore not surprizing that special importance was given to Arabic in the Deccan by the Bahmanids. Maḥmūd Shāh (d. 1397) himself was a poet and patron of Arabic studies. His successor Fīrōz Shah used to send ships every year from the ports of Goa and Chaul to bring celebrated scholars and poets from the Arabic speaking world to the residence Gulbarga. His brother built a special college for Gīsūdarāz who, in addition to his manifold activities as mystical leader, commentator and translator wrote simple religious Arabic poetry.

Under the Quṭbshāhī dynasty of Golconda (1512–1687), Arabic studies gained even more importance. The Quṭbshāhī kings who were of Shia persuasion spoke Telugu among themselves, but went to great lengths to attract Arabic scholars and poets to their court; one may especially mention the philosopher Niẓāmuddīn Gīlānī (d. 1649) *ḥakīm al-mulk*, a disciple of the Persian thinker Mīr Dāmād.[35]

The most interesting development, however, is that of Arabic poetry at the court. Amīr Sayyid Aḥmad ibn Ma'ṣūm came from Mecca at the invitation of Muḥammad Qulī Quṭbshāh whose daughter he married in 1045. He died in

---

[32] GAL II 220, S II 309; ZA p. 17ff., 23ff.; II 2, III 13, V 4, IX 6, X 2.

[33] Printed Lucknow 1306 h. GAL S II 610; ZA 23ff., I 11, IV 21, IX 19; a similar work in undotted letters dealing with Sufism and ethics was composed by Faiḍī under the title *mawārid al-kilam wa silk durar al-ḥikam* (Calcutta 1241 h/1825.) ZA 19 mentions another attempt at writing a commentary of the Quran in an unusual way, e.g. 'Abdulaḥad's *ǧab šaǵab*, finished 1307 h./1889, which consists exclusively of dotted letters but comprises only the last part (*ǧuz' 'ammā*) of the Quran.

[34] For the whole problem cf. M. A. Muid Khan, The Arabian Poets of Golconda, Bombay 1963.

[35] ZA VI 11.

prison in 1674 after a futile attempt to gain the throne. His main poetic works are *qaṣīdas* in honour of his royal father-in-law in the style of classical Arabic poetry, which lack none of the well-known features used for the last thousand years in Bedouin poetry. Similar are the verses of other poets who, hailing from Iraq, Yemen, Syria and Egypt and attracted by Sayyid Aḥmad's fame, came to Golconda. The greatest poet among them is without doubt Sayyid Aḥmad's own son Sayyid ʿAlī[36] (d. 1705 in Shiraz) who joined his father in later days. His poetical description of his journey from his hometown Mecca to India (*salwat al-ġarīb* 'Consolation of the Stranger') is as much worth exploring as his *sulāfat al-ʿaṣr* 'The Best Wine of the Century,' a biographical work on contemporary Arabic writers in a period which has been studied, until now, in Europe only at random. Sayyid ʿAlī wrote every kind of poetry, from winesongs to elegies, and his style is in general as traditional as his father's. Yet, he also used now and then strophic forms which were particularly popular in his days in Yemen. His rhetorical skill induced him to compose a poem of 155 verses in which every conceivable rhetorical device is applied.

One has to keep in mind, however, that Persian literature—especially historiography—flourished in the Deccan as well;[37] but to appreciate this literature, one has to turn, first, to the historical development of the Persian literature written in the Subcontinent.

As already observed, its amount is far more extensive than that composed in Iran proper.[38] Yet Indo-Persian literature has rarely attracted the interest of Western students, and even an outstanding master of Persian poetry in India such as Ġālib (d. 1869) was sure that the products of Indo-Persian poets (with the exception of his own verses, of course!) were inferior to those of the poets of Iran. Only the indigenous historians received early attention in the West; the British have depended largely upon Indo-Persian historiography in reconstructing the history of Muslim rule in India.

There is not a single branch of Persian literature lacking in the Subcontinent. The subjects range from high-flown mystical poetry to biographies and medical treatises, giving us a full picture of the cultural life during almost 900 years. The literary forms developed in Iran were accepted in India, too: Muslims, and from the 15th century Hindus as well, used the *qaṣīda* (long poem of praise), the lyrical *ġazal*, the *qiṭʿa* ('fragment,' e.g. a *ġazal* in which the first two hemi-

---

[36] GAL II 421, S II 627; ZA IV 35, VIII 12, IX 34.

[37] Abdul Karim Husaini, Persian Language in the Deccan, Hyderabad 1934; Kalām ul-mulūk, ed. Mir Saʿadat Ali Rizwi, Hyderabad 1357 (Persian poetry written by the Bahmani, ʿAdilshahi, and Qutbshahi kings).

[38] General Surveys: Iqbal Husain, Early Persian Poets of India, Patna s.d.; M. A. Ghani, Premughal Persian Literature in Hindostan, Allahabad s.d.; Shibli Nuʿmani, šiʿr al-ʿağam, 5 vols, Cawnpore 1920–23 (in Urdu); J. Marek, Persian Literature in India, in R 713–734, 843–38 (bibliography); S. M. Ikram, Armaġān-i Pāk, Karachi [2]1953 (a useful anthology of Persian poetry written in the Subcontinent).

stiches do not rhyme), and *rubā'ī* (quatrain) with equal ease, skilfully applying the Arabo-Persian meters and the monorhyme. The *munāẓara*, 'tenzone,' poetically describing a disputation between two items—pen and sword, hemp and wine, etc.—common in Iran since the early 11th century, was introduced by 'Amīd Dailamī in the mid 13th century. Frequently used was the long epical poem in rhyming couplets, *maṯnawī*, for which only seven strictly limited meters of at the most 11 syllables were permitted; use of these was restricted according to the subject matter. Shorter poems in rhyming couplets were often called *sāqīnāme* because they usually began with the invocation of the cupbearer, *sāqī*. The art of literary riddles (*mu'ammà, luġz*) and logogriphs was very popular.[39] In the religious sphere one finds *madḥ* and *na't*, praise of God or the Prophet respectively, both in *qaṣīdas* and in the introduction of *maṯnawī*'s. The *manqibat* tells of the miracles of the Prophet, the Shia *imāms* or Sufi saints; the *marṯiya*, a threnody about the martyrdom of Ḥusain, the Prophet's grandson, in the battle of Kerbela (10 Muḥarram 680) was mainly elaborated in 19th century Urdu poetry. Like the Turks, the Indian Muslims were fond of the art of producing *ta'rīḫ* 'chronograms' from meaningful words or sentences (since each Arabic letter has a numerical value); in many cases the title of a book gives, in its numerical value, the date of its completion.

F. Rückert's excellent work *Grammatik, Poetik und Rhetorik der Perser* (1827), gives a good impression of the artistic side of the Persian poetry in the Subcontinent[40]—all the more, since this study is a German adaptation of one of the first books ever type-printed in India, i.e. the *Haft Qulzum* 'Seven Oceans' by Qabūl Muḥammad which was completed in Lucknow under the auspices of Ḥaidar Shah in 1821.

Not only the form but also the imagery of Persian literature was taken over in India, although the first specimens of Indo-Persian poetry date back to a time when the poetical art was not yet fully developed in Iran proper. Nevertheless the constant interplay of contrasting pairs of concepts (such as Beauty and Love, Rose and Nightingale, Turk and Hindu, etc.) as well as the rhetorical figure called *ḥusn-i ta'līl* 'phantastic aetiology' and similar devices permeated Persian poetry from its very beginning. In judging the achievements of the Indo-Persian poets we have to keep in mind the tradition-bound character of Persian poetry in which the true art consists not in the expression of personal feelings but rather in more and more exquisite and exotic elaborations of set topics. The elaboration of the subtleties of meter and the elegant use of rhyme form part of this highly intellectual art. The invention of far-fetched *concetti* in which the inherited imagery is ornamented in surprising ways seems to have been the main occupation of many later Persian-writing poets.

[39] About riddles and logogriphs cf. E 345. Some writers, like Faiḍī, even composed riddles about the Most Beautiful Names of God.

[40] F. Rückert, Grammatik, Poetik und Rhetorik der Perser, 1827, ed. W. Pertsch, Berlin 1872; repr. 1966. A most ingenious chronogram on Dārā Shikoh's wedding—1043 h.—on p. 246ff.

The *naẓīra*, the emulation of a classical model,[41] is one peculiar artistic play—suffice it to mention the almost innumerable imitations of Niẓāmī's *Ḫamsa* 'Quintet' or parts of it, each epic composed invariably according to the meter of the original poem. Thus all the *maṯnawī*'s composed after Niẓāmī's *maḫzan al-asrār* 'Treasure of Mysteries' are not only written in the same meter (i.e. *sarī*') as the original but usually bear also titles rhyming in *ār*, like Amīr Ḫosrau's *maṭla*' *al-anwār*, Ğihāngīr Hāšimī's *maẓhar al-āṯār*, and more than seventy others.[42] The 'response' to a famous *ġazal* or *qaṣīda* became increasingly common in later times so that it is not difficult to find the sources of almost all the Persian *qaṣīdas* by Ġālib as well as for many of his Persian *ġazals*.

One of the first names of an author writing in Persian in the Subcontinent is that of Rābi'a al-Quzdārīya, a woman from Quzdar at the border of Sind and Balochistan who composed a few poems in early Ghaznawid time and became herself the heroine of later poetry.[43]

During early Ghaznawid days, shortly after the year 1000, Lahore became the centre of Muslim learning. Here, the first Persian work on Sufism was composed: the *kašf al-maḥǧūb* 'The Unveiling of what is Veiled' which belongs to the most important sources of early Islamic mysticism in its sober approach;[44] its author, Huǧwīrī (d. ca. 1071) called Datā Ganǧ Baḫš, is still venerated by the Panjabis as a great saint.

He says in his discussion of faith *(īmān)*:

"Hence in reality, without any controversy among Muslims, faith is gnosis and acknowledgment and acceptance of works. Whoever knows God knows Him by one of His attributes, and the most elect of His attributes are of three kinds: those connected with His beauty *(ǧamāl)*, and with His majesty *(ǧalāl)* and with His perfection *(kamāl)*" (R. A. Nicholson, p. 288).

Other Persian works of this mystic, who hailed from Ghazna, are unfortunately lost. That Maḥmūd of Ghazna, the conqueror of North West India, should become converted by—mostly mystically inclined—poets into the model of the 'great lover' enamoured with his Turkish slave Ayāz, is one of the most unexpected developments in Persian poetry.[45]

---

[41] Cf. E 245ff. with an impressive number of *naẓīras* written to Niẓāmī's Ḫamsa between the 13th and 19th centuries; id. 231 an enumeration of *naẓīra's* of Ğāmī's Yūsuf ū Zulaiḫā.

[42] Cf. Ahmad 'Ali Ahmad (Storey Nr. 1224), taḏkira-yi Haft Asmān, Calc. 1873, repr. Teheran 1965.

[43] Cf. 'Aufi, lubāb al-albāb II 61; M. Ishaque, Four Eminent Poetesses of Iran, Calcutta 1950; S. Safa, ta'rīḫ-i adabiyāt-i Īrān, Teheran 1338 s, 449ff.; F. Meier, Die schöne Mahsati, Wiesbaden 1963, 27ff.; H. Massé, The Poetess Rābi'a Gozdarī, in: Yādnāma-yi Jan Rypka, Prague 1967.

[44] Ed. V. A. Žukovskij, Leningrad 1926; translated by R. A. Nicholson: The kashf al-maḥjūb, the oldest Persian Treatise on Sufism of'Alī ibn 'Uthmān al-Jullabī al-Hujwīrī, London 1911, repr. 1959.

[45] Cf. G. Spies, Maḥmūd von Ghazna bei Farīduddīn 'Aṭṭār, Basel 1959. Epics about Maḥmūd and Ayāz: E 250. P. Hardy, Mahmud of Ghazna and the Historians, BSOAS March 1963 (Lahore 1963).

'Aufī, in his *lubāb al-albāb*, mentions a surprising number of poets who flourished in Lahore (called 'little Ghazna') as panegyrists of the Ghaznawid rulers. The first of these poets was 'Abdallāh ibn Rūzbih al-Lāhōrī in the time of Mas'ūd, Maḥmūd Ghaznawī's son (d. 1040). But it was Abū'l-Farağ Rūnī (d. 1091) who marked the beginning of great poetry in Muslim India.[46] He spent most of his life in Lahore, and his eulogies of the later Ghaznawids gained him wide fame; even the noted Persian panegyrist Anwarī (d. ca. 1189) admired him, saying: 'It may be known that I am the slave of the poetry of Abū'l-Farağ!'—Rūnī's few charming *ġazals* contain a considerable number of those motifs that were later considered characteristic for the *ġazal*: beautiful plays on words that still do not veil the meaning, complaints about the faithlessness of Time and of the beloved, admiration for the beauty of the cute youthful beloved, etc.

The leading poet of this early period is Mas'ūd ibn Sa'd-i Salmān (1046–ca. 1131), a wealthy landlord who was imprisoned at the age of ca. 40 years because he interfered in politics. After his release toward the end of the 11th century, he was made governor of Jhalandar but was once more imprisoned; 1107 he was set free and lived to an old age. Sanā'ī, the mystical poet from Ghazna (d. ca. 1131), carefully collected his verses.[47]—Mas'ūd's fame rests mainly upon his *ḥabsiyāt*, poems he sent from his prison in the fortress Nāy to the ruler—from this time, the category of prison-poems is frequently found in Indo-Muslim literature: ranging from Amīr Faḫruddīn 'Amīd Sinnāmī's (d. ca. 1283) more artificial verses to Ġālib's beautiful Persian strophic poems which are among his finest works, not to mention the numerous *ḥabsiyāt* written during the British rule and finally, in our day, those in Urdu by Fayz Ahmad Fayz.—It seems that Mas'ūd also composed poetry of the so-called *šahr-āšūb*-type, complaining about the cruel beloved who appears in various professional guises—a form which serves the poet to introduce into his verses technical terms, like those of the butcher, the Sufi, the amberseller, the cobbler, etc.; the form itself was used later to complain about the vicissitudes of fate and the destruction which had overcome the different trades and crafts.—Another, often overlooked feature of Mas'ūd's poetry is the introduction of the 'month-poem' *bārāmāsa*, into Persian: this genre, derived from Sanskrit poetry dealing with the aspects of the seasons,[48] became very popular in Muslim poetry in the regional languages, like Sindhi, Panjabi, and especially Bengali, though in Persian is was scarcely ever imitated. Mas'ūd ibn Sa'd used the Persian months —beginning with Naurūz on March 21, to extol his ruler, cleverly connecting the different seasons with wine and pleasure.—Mas'ūd's style is still comparatively simple. He excells in using unpretentious language and almost colloquial

---

[46] Dīvān, ed. M. M. Damġānī, Teheran 1348 s.; cf. E 256.

[47] Dīvān, ed. R. Yāšmī, Teheran s.d.; cf. E 256–7; R 196; Sanā'ī's poem on the occasion of his collection of Mas'ūd's poetry in: Dīvān-i Ḥakīm Sanā'ī, ed. M. Riżawī, Teheran 1341 š. p. 1060.

[48] Cf. D. H. H. Ingalls, Sanscrit Poetry from Vidyakara's 'Treasury', Cambridge, Mass. 1968.

sentences to produce a highly artistic effect, and both his *qaṣīdas* and his short *rubā'īyāt*—a genre which was becoming very fashionable during that period—show him to be a master of concise formulation. The touching contents of his *ḥabsiyāt* never cease to appeal to the reader. He proudly addresses his home-town with ever new questions, contrasting its old glorious state with its present misery, after he has been carried away:

"O Lahore, woe to you!—without me, how are you?
Without the radiant sun,—how are you? . . .
You were a meadow, and I the lion of the meadow—
How have you been with me, and how are you without me? . . .
Your lap becomes emptied of friends, one by one—
With hidden foes in the skirt—how are you? . . ."

And he complains:

"The mountain, upon which affliction is loaded—that's me.
The sword which was given in the hand of grief—that's me.
The lion, who is not left out (of the cage)—that's me.
The abject one who is well kept—that's me."

As soon as Muslim rule in Northwestern India was firmly established, historical writing—a branch of literature and scholarship particularly dear to the Muslims everywhere—began to develop in the Subcontinent.[49] The first remarkable works of historical interest were composed in Sind during the governorship of Nāṣiraddīn Qabāča before his stronghold Bhakkar was conquered in 1228 by Iltutmish, the ruler of Delhi. In that very city of Bhakkar 'Alī al-Kūfī, a scholar from Ucch, found in the late 12th century an Arabic manuscript about the history of Sind in pre-Islamic and early Islamic times. 'He took the book out of the veil of Arabic and brought it into Persian.'[50] Its title is usually given as *Čačnāme*, but should be rather *fatḥnāme-yi Sind* 'Book of the conquest of Sind.' This historical work appears to have drawn largely upon al-Madā'inī's (d. ca. 840) lost *futūḥ al-Hind wa's-Sind*, and thus conveys a good picture of early Arabic historiography.

When the pressure of the Mongols in Central Asia and the Eastern fringe of Khorassan grew stronger, a number of scholars and poets found shelter in Sind. One of them was Muḥammad 'Aufī who reached the country, after long journeying, in 1220.[51] His *lubāb al-albāb* 'Quintessence of the Hearts' dedicated to

[49] About Indo-Muslim historical writing cf. the translations and excerpts in H. Elliot and J. Dowson, The History of India as told by its own Historians 1867ff.; further E 361; Storey p. 425–780; F. Tauer in R 448ff.; C. H. Philips, Historians of India, Pakistan, and Ceylon, London 1961; Khan Bahadur Maulvi Zafar Hasan, Bibliography of Indo-Moslem History excluding Provincial Monarchies, Calcutta 1932.

[50] Ed. M. U. Daudpota, Delhi 1939; Sindhi translation Karachi 1954, Urdu translation Hyderabad/Sind 1963; partial translation by T. Postans, JRAS Bengal 1838; History of Sind in two parts . . . transl. from Persian books by Mirza Kalichbeg Fredunbeg, Karachi 1901; Storey p. 650f.

[51] Ed. E. G. Browne and Mirza Muhammad of Kazwin, London-Leyden 1903, 1906; ed. S. Nafīsī, Teheran 1333–35 s.; M. Nizamuddin, Introduction to the

Qabāča's vizier Faḫraddīn al-Ḥusainī, contains notes about nearly 300 poets and was the first book about literary figures during the Ghaznawid and Ghorid period. Although lacking exact information about the dates, the *lubāb* is an indispensable source for the history of early Persian poetry, especially, as it was written by a poet (who also composed *qaṣīdas*, called *madā'iḥ as-sulṭān*). The *lubāb al-albāb* inaugurated a whole literature of biographies of poets.—'Aufī's second book, *ǧawāmi' al-ḥikāyāt* 'Necklaces of Anecdotes . . .' a collection of about 2000 anecdotes in 25 chapters which has been translated into Turkish several times, was planned at Qabāča's request, but after his fall dedicated to Iltutmish's vizier Qiwāmuddīn Muḥammad in 1230. It is a veritable mine of information about folklore and literary traditions of the early 13th century.

Numerous poets adorned Qabāča's court in Ucch, and there flourished another historical writer, Minhāǧ as-Sirāǧ (d. 1260) who, like 'Aufī, later left Sind for Delhi which was soon to become the new seat of culture. Minhāǧ's *ṭabaqāt-i Nāṣirī* display his detailed personal knowledge of contemporary events, for he had been closely associated with the Ghorids.[52]—The literary interest almost takes precedence over the historical one in Ḥasan Niẓāmī's *tāǧ al-ma'āṯir* 'Crown of Memorials,' a verbose and rhetorical historical work that deals principally with Quṭbaddīn Aibak's rule (1206–10), although without neglecting his predecessors and successors. The author has been called 'a truthful narrator without any axe to grind.'[53]

Slightly after Niẓāmī, Faḫr-i Mudabbir composed his *ādāb al-ḥarb wa'š-šaǧā'a* which, as its title indicates, deals in part with instruments of warfare but is actually more a kind of Fürstenspiegel illustrating the duties of the good rulers and the ruling classes with quotations from the Quran, traditions, and classical Persian lore. This approach is typical for 'Mirrors of Princes,' a genre that had flourished in Iran around 1100. Faḫri has also composed an extensive genealogical work, beginning with Adam and Eve.[54]

The best histories of the Delhi Sultanate were composed in the 14th century The outstanding scholar in this field is Ḍiyā'uddīn Baranī (ca. 1285–after 1360) who wrote mainly under Muḥammad ibn Tughluq (1325–52) whose *nadīm* (convive) he seems to have been. Under Fīrōzshah Tughluq he was imprisoned for a while. His main work is the *ta'rīḫ-i Fīrōzšāhī*.[55] Baranī has been called 'a rank reactionary in politics and a die-hard conservative in religion.' Indeed

---

Jawāmi'ul-Hikāyāt wa Lawāmi'ur-Riwāyāt, a critical Study of its Scope, Sources, and Values. London 1929. Cf. E 332; Storey Nr. 1088; R 222; Marek/R 715; E. G. Browne, A Literary History of Persia I 477ff.

[52] Ed. W. Nassau Lees, Khadim Husain and Abdul Hayy, Calcutta 1864, transl. H. G. Raverty, Calcutta 1897; Storey Nr. 104; Tauer/R 439.

[53] Cf. Storey Nr. 664; Tauer/R 449.

[54] Ed. A. S. Khwānsarī, Teheran 1967; Ta'rīḫ-i Fakhru'd-Dīn Mubārakshāh . . . ed. Denison Ross, London 1927; Abdus Sattar Khan, Fakhr-i Mudabbir, IC 1938; Storey Nr. 1644.

[55] Ta'rīh-i Firozšāhī, ed. Sir Sayyid Ahmad Khan, Calcutta 1860–62; part. translation by P. Whalleys, JASBengal 1871; for his *fatāwā-i ǧahāndārī* cf. M.

his description of events is rather biassed, for he had clear-cut ideals of how a king should behave. Thus he praised rulers who enforced the laws of the *šarī'a*, and those like Nāṣiruddīn ibn Iltutmish who wrote Qurans and lived on the money he gained from his calligraphy; other sultans are cursed because of the debauchery prevailing during their reign. Baranī's style is forceful and impressive, and his books which say much in favour of the mystical leaders, show the wide gap between medieval politics and religious practices.[56] His discussion of the vices of the low-born proves his 'reactionary' attitude quite well:

> "The majority of *ḥakīms* and wise men, ancient and modern, have said on the basis of observation and experience that the great offices appertaining to the administration have not been well discharged by the low-born and the base. If a base-born man has become a ruler, he has striven so far as he could to overthrow men of good birth and to elevate the low-born and the base. The ultimate work of the low-born has never come to any good, and they have never shown loyalty in any contingency. Though owing to the flattery, agility, display of intelligence and jugglery of the low-born and the mean, some sultans have been captivated and have made such people their colleagues and the confidential officers of the kingdom. Yet both during their life-time and after their death they have suffered such wounds and injuries from the low-born men they have promoted that regret for what they did will not diminish in their minds through all eternity." (K. A. Nizami, Some Aspects . . ., p. 109).

Almost contemporary with Baranī is 'Iṣāmī who composed an epical poem *futūḥ as-salāṭīn*, that tells the history of Muslim India since the Ghaznawids.[57] He dedicated his epic to Abū'l-Muẓaffar Bahman Shah, the first ruler of the Bahmanid dynasty in the Deccan. For 'Iṣāmī himself had been transplanted to the Deccan by Muhammad Tughluq's edict that forced large parts of the Delhi population in 1327 to leave the capital and settle in Daulatabad, the veritable geographical centre of the kingdom.

As to the Bahmanid court is became soon a centre of learning (vd. supra) where, towards the end of the century Šaiḫ Āḏarī Isfarā'īnī wrote his *Bahmannāme* in Persian verses. And the tradition established by 'Iṣāmī continued through the centuries—the last epical poem of this kind is Mollā Fīrōz ibn Kāūs' *Ǧurǧnāme* '(King) George's Book' which relates in 40000 couplets the history of India up to 1817. . .[58]

Again in the end of the 14th century (apparently after Timur's invasion of Northwest India in 1398) Šams-i Sirāǧ 'Afīf in Delhi wrote his *ta'rīḫ Fīrōzšāhī*;[59] Firoz Shah Tughluq himself is credited with a briefish account of his

Habib and Dr. Afsar Afzalu'-dDin, The political Theory of the Delhi Sultanate, Aligarh 1960; cf. Storey Nr. 669; Tauer/R 449.

[56] Cf. Aziz Ahmad, Trends in Political Thought of Medieval Muslim India, Stud. Isl. XVII, 1962.

[57] Agha Mahdi Hasan, Isami's futūḥu's-salāṭīn, the Shahname of Medieval India, Agra 1938; ed. A. S. Usha, Madras 1948; E 236; Storey Nr. 612; Tauer/R 448.

[58] E 238; MM 1307; ed. Bombay 1837. About the development of historical epics in India cf. E 237f.

[59] Ed. Maulvi Wilayat Husain, Calcutta 1888–90; Storey Nr. 669; Tauer/R 449.

own reign in which he emphasizes his mildness, his passion for building, etc.[60]

The works of these historians and of some less important writers give a comparatively good picture of the situation in India during early Muslim times but should not be regarded as the only sources available. The verses of a poet like Amīr Ḫosrau or the notebooks and table-talks of the mystical leaders often contribute more to our knowledge of the social problems and everyday life than court historiography and official documents.

Especially the activities of Muslim mystics constitute a most important aspect of medieval Indian literature. Some members of two great mystical orders had reached the Subcontinent in the late 12th century: Mu'īnuddīn Čištī (d. 1236) settled in Ajmer, the heart of Rajputana.[61] From here the Sufi order of the Chishtiya, renowned for its ascetic practices but also for its love of poetry and music, spread all over India. The first centre of the Suhrawardiya was Multan, the seat of Bahā'uddīn Zakariya, the mystical master of one of the most fascinating authors of Persian mystical love poetry, Faḫruddīn 'Irāqī (d. 1283). This poet who stayed for 25 years with Bahā'uddīn, wrote musical *ġazals* still to be heard in Multan.[62]—The Suhrawardiya sent their missionaries as far as East Bengal where the order continued to flourish throughout the centuries without, however, contributing to any great extent to mystic poetry. In the Čištī tradition, on the other hand, poetry was highly esteemed. The first great poet in this line was Quṭb Ǧamāluddīn Aḥmad Hānswī (d. 1260),[63] one of the *ḫalīfas* of Farīduddīn Ganǧ-i Šakar of Pakpattan (d. 1265).[64] His Persian mystical verses are sweet and unassuming, sometimes slightly didactic and not as ecstatic as those of this contemporary 'Irāqī whose enthusiastic love surpassed all limits in his jubilant songs. A more emotional note is found in the work of the next known poet from the Pakpattan environment, Shāh Bū 'Alī Qalandar (d. 1323). His eulogy celebrating the Prophet's birth introduces this form, so common in the central Islamic world, into the Subcontinent.

"Welcome, O Nightingale of the Ancient Garden,
Speak to us about the Lovely Rose!
Welcome, our flying Messenger—
Every moment you give news from our Friend!
Welcome, O Hoepoe of happy augury!
Welcome, O sugar-talking Parrot! . . ."

[60] Ed. Dehli 1885, Aligarh 1954(?)

[61] Storey Nr. 943; MM 1298; cf. E 365 about Persian histories of the Čištīya up to the 18th century; further the bibliography in: K. A. Nizami, Some Aspects of Religion and Politics in India during the 13th century, Bombay 1961.

[62] Browne, Literary History II 124ff.; R 254; Kulliyāt, ed. S. Nafīsī, Teheran 1338 s.; The Book of the Lovers, ed. and transl. by A. J. Arberry, Oxford 1939; Y. D. Ahuja, Iraqi in India, IC 1958.

[63] Dīvān, Delhi 1889; K. V. Zetterstéen, Selection from the Diwan of Jamāluddīn Aḥmad Hānsawī, Isl. Research Ass. Misc., Vol. I 1948. About his Arabic *mulhamāt*, Alwar 1306 h/1889 cf. ZA III 1.

[64] K. A. Nizami, The Life and Times of Shaikh Farīdu'd-Dīn Ganj Shakar, Aligarh 1955; his conversations asrār-i auliyā', ed. Badr Ishaq, Lucknow 1917.

His enraptured verses about Divine love are not so overburdened with mystical terminology as are the poems of many later poets who filled their simple lines with high-flown pseudo-philosophical concepts. But Bū 'Alī Qalandar is also known as the author of some forceful letters to the rulers of Delhi, following the true Čištī-tradition which keeps aloof from worldly power in order to maintain independence.

Bū 'Alī was a contemporary of the greatest poet medieval Muslim India produced—Amīr Ḫosrau.[65] Like Bū 'Alī, the latter was a member of the Čištīya order, but much more a courtier and gentleman than a genuine mystic, notwithstanding his close friendship with the leading Čištī saint of his time, Niẓāmuddīn Auliyā' of Delhi. Amīr Ḫosrau, born in 1253 in Patyala as the son of a Turkish officer and a mother of Indian extraction, displayed his poetic talent very early. His master in poetry was Šihābuddīn Maḥmira Badā'ūnī who had written, in addition to the usual panegyrics, delicate religious poetry. Ḫosrau accompanied several princes to various places in the Subcontinent, from Bengal to Multan, and had to endure imprisonment by the Mongols who had reached the outskirts of North West India in 1284. He went, then, to Oudh, returned to Delhi in 1289, and died there in 1325, having sung the praises of at least seven rulers. Yet, one should not blame the 'parrot of India' or 'God's Turk' *(turk Allāh)* too much for his shifting allegiances to rulers who were often deadly enemies (though generally good connoisseurs of poetry)—his was the journalistic approach to power which is so typical of many *hommes-de-lettres* in the medieval East. The ease with which he wrote enabled him to turn his pen to ever new subjects. Musician and scholar, mystic and panegyrist, he was as good in lyrics as in highly complicated prose and could easily emulate all styles of poetry as they had developed up to his time in Iran, from Ḫāqānī's complicated and forceful *qaṣīdas* to Niẓāmī's romantic *maṯnawīs*. His contribution to the form of *ġazal*, hitherto not too frequently used in India, is significant. His knowledge of Arabic, Turkish, and Hindi—in addition to Persian—gave him the possibility of introducing most exotic wordplays and stunning literary devises into his verses; W. Berthels is certainly right to speak of his 'powdered style.'

He uses the Indian motif of the rainy season as connected with love and happiness, turning it in a delicate way:

"The cloud weeps, and I become separated from my friend—
How can I separate my heart from my heart's friend on such a day?
The cloud weeping—and I and the friend standing, bidding farewell—
I weeping separately, the cloud separately, the friend separately . . ."

He is very fond of joining two apparently contrasting facts in order to describe the inexplicable magic of love:

---

[65] Waheed Mirza, Amir Khosrau, Calcutta 1935, Allahabad 1949; Elliot, History of India III 524–66; M. Habib, Life of Amir Khusro, Bombay 1927; E 244f.; R 257ff.; Naqi M. Khan Khurjavi, Ḥayāt-i Khusrau, Karachi 1956; M. Mo'in, Amīr Khusrau Dihlawi, Īrān ū Hind I, 1952.

"You carried the soul from (my) body—and yet, you are still in the soul;
You have given pains—and are still the remedy;
Openly you split my breast—
Yet, you are still hidden in my heart.
You have destroyed the kingdom of my heart with the sword of coquetry.
And are still a ruler in that ruined place . . . "

One of his most frequently quoted *ġazals* is the love-song—composed in a lovely light meter with many short syllables—in which he hopes that his beloved should quicken him by granting him a kiss, thus exchanging his nostalgic soul for another one (as traditional imagery has it very often):

"Tonight there came a news that you, o beloved, would come—
Be my head sacrificed to the road along which you will come riding!
All the gazelles of the desert have put their heads on their hands
In the hope that one day you will come to hunt them . . .
My soul has come on my lip (e.g. I am on the point of expiring); come, so that I may remain alive—
After I am no longer—for what purpose will you come?"

And his ingenious way of treating Arabic is understood from a verse taken from a praise-poem in which he plays upon homonymes:

"He is fountain *('ain)* of modesty, nay, his eye *('ain)* is the embodiment *('ain)* of modesty;
He is an ocean of generosity, nay his hand (*kaf*, also: 'foam') is identical *('ain)* with the ocean."

According to Firišta, Amīr Ḫosrau composed 92 books.[66] Even though this may be an exaggeration, the number of his extant books is quite impressive. There are his five lyrical *dīvāns* (he collected the poetry of different stages of his life in separate *dīvāns*, whereas most poets, or their disciples for them, published their poems in a single collection); further a *Ḫamsa*, i.e. five *maṯnawīs* written in emulation of Niẓāmī, which were often illustrated in later times,[67] and also a number of historical *maṯnawīs* which give a vivid picture of Indian

[66] Editions: Dīvān-i kāmil, ed. S. Nafīsī ū M. Darvīsh, Teheran 1343 š.; Maǧnūn Lailā, ed. G. A. Magerramov, Moscow 1964; Širīn Ḫusrau, ed. Haji Ali Ahmad Khan, Aligarh 1927 ed G. Alijef, Moscow 1961; maṭla' al-anwār, Lucknow 1884; qirān as-sa'dain Lucknow 1885, ed. Maulvi Mohd. Isma'il, Aligarh 1918; Duwal Rānī Ḫiḍr Ḫān, ed. R. A. Salim, Aligarh 1917; Hašt Bihišt, ed. Maulana Sulaiman Ashraf, Aligarh 1918; Nuh Sipihr, ed. Waheed Mirza, Calcutta 1948; Tuǧluqnāma, ed. S. Hashmi Faridabadi, Aurangabad 1933; Ḫazā'in al-futūḥ, ed. Aligarh 1927, ed. Waheed Mirza, Calcutta 1953; transl. M. Habib, The Campaigns of Alā'ud-dīn Khalji, Madras 1931; Ā'inayi Sikandarī, ed. Maulana Sa'id Ahmad Faruqi, Aligarh 1917.

[67] About illustrations cf. J. Stchoukine, B. Flemming, P. Luft, H. Sohrweide, Illuminierte Islamische Handschriften (Verz. der Orient. Hss. in Deutschland), Wiesbaden 1971 Nr. 27 and Nr. 62, the latter a copy from the library of Khankhanan 'Abdurraḥīm; Chester Beatty Library, Catalogue of the Persian Mss. and miniatures, Dublin 1960ff., Nr. 163, 226; also R. Ettinghausen, Pre-Mughal Painting in India, Trudy Congr. Vostokovedov, Moskau 1964 IV 191, and almost every publication on Persian and Mughal Painting.

life and customs around 1300. His *maṯnawī qirān as-sa'dain* deals with the meeting of Sultan Mu'izzuddīn Kaikobād with his father Bughrā Khān 1289; Fīrōzshāh Khiljī's victories were described in *miftāḥ al-futūḥ*; 'Alā'uddīn Khiljī's achievements were celebrated in the prose work *ḫazā'in al-futūḥ*. The *maṯnawī Duwal Rānī Ḫiḍr Ḫān* ends with the marriage of 'Alā'uddīn's son Khiḍr Khān after a description of Delhi, and of 'Alā'uddīn's wars against Gujrat and Malwa. The *Tuġluqnāma* was written in honour of Ghiyāthuddīn Tughluq, and the *Nuh Sipihr*, 'Nine Spheres' is poetically interesting since its nine chapters are written in a different meter each.[68]

Since Amīr Ḫosrau knew the country from East to West, his writings contain many hints to Indian customs, fruits, festivals and dresses. India is, for him, the earthly paradise: was not Adam exiled to India, and are not the peacock and the serpent, both connected with legends about Paradise, animals of India?

It is highly possible that Amīr Ḫosrau may have written treatises on music, but they seem to have been lost—in any case, his role as the inaugurator of the Indo-Muslim musical style, and as inventor of several instruments is well known. Thus he is credited with the invention of *tarāna* and *ḫiyāl* as poetical forms meant for singing. It is therefore small wonder that his lyrics are well suited for singing and still belong to the standard repertoire of every good musician of the classical North Indian style. Amir Ḫosrau was also the first in India to compose treatises on epistolography, *inšā'*, an art which had flourished in the Near East since Abbasid days.[69] These handbooks are important sources for our knowledge of cultural life, since they show not only details of the court protocol but also reveal many otherwise unknown aspects of daily life. In these works, Amīr Ḫosrau has shown the styles to be used in dealing with the various strata of population so that we get a vivid impression of the flexibility of Persian during the early 14th century and become acquainted with some of the problems with which a court official had to cope. His example was followed by many other writers the most important of whom was Maḥmūd Gawān (executed 1481) at the Bahmanid court who acted during 35 years as minister under four kings.[70] His books on various topics, mainly his *riyāḍ al-insā'* are of paramount value, and the great Persian poet Ǧāmī of Herat (d. 1492) dedicated to him a well-known poem and made use of his letters.

A special genre in Indo-Muslim literature are the 'letters of guidance' written by Sufi leaders to their disciples. The form is not novel—the mystics in 10th century Bagdad had composed similar letters. In India, however, these collections, beginning with that of Ḥamīduddīn Nāgōrī (d. 1274)

[68] About the problems of Indo-Muslim Epics cf. Aziz Ahmad, Epic and Counter-epic in Medieval India, JAOS 84/4, 1963.

[69] Publ. Lucknow 1876; cf. S. H. Askari, Rasā'il ul-i'jāz of Amīr Khusrau, an appraisal, Zakir Husain Vol., Delhi 1967, 116ff.;—About the development of official correspondence in India cf. E 338 Tauer/R 434.

[70] riyāḍ ul-inšā', ed. Ustad Shaikh Chand, Hyderabad 1948; E 339.

were of special importance, for often they were written with not only the addressee in mind but were meant for wider circulation. Thus we can gather from them more information about the teachings of some Sufis than is possible from many theoretical works. The tradition of letter-writing continued through the ages—Aḥmad Sirhindī, the Muslim revivalist Sufi in the early 17th century, gained his fame mainly through his 524 letters, and even in the 19th century Ġālib wrote his letters with the aim of having them one day published.

Another important type of Persian writing produced among the Sufis came into existence around 1300: the *malfūẓāt*, collections of sayings of spiritual masters, gathered by their faithful disciples[71]. The first important example is the *fawā'id al-fu'ād* 'Things profitable to the Heart' by the poet Ḥasan Siğzī Dihlawī[72] who recorded Niẓāmuddīn Auliyā's conversations between 1307 and 1322. The *ḫair al-mağālis* 'Best of Meetings' of Niẓāmuddīn's successor Čirāġ-i Dihlawī, compiled by Maulānā Ḥāmid Qalandar and carefully revised by the master, has provided one of the most frequently used sources for later hagiographies in Muslim India.—Worth mentioning is the *siyar al-auliyā'* by Muḥammad Mubārak Kirmānī Mīr Ḫūrd, a biographical work by a Čištī mystic who had to migrate to the Deccan in 1327. In order to atone for deserting his master's tomb in Delhi (albeit under government pressure) he wrote this account which contains very important information about early Čištī life in India, and set the model of numerous biographies of saints to follow.[73] We may also mention the *ma'dan al-ma'ānī* 'Mine of Inner Meanings' by Šarafuddīn Aḥmad al-Manērī (d. 1380), a Bihari saint known as well as the author of several didactic books on Sufism and impressive letters.[74] The genre of *malfūẓāt* became so popular that forgeries were produced for pious purposes in later times.

Among the early poets of the Čištīya, the most outstanding personality is the compiler of the *fawā'id al-fu'ād*, Ḥasan Siğzī Dihlawī, a friend of Amīr Ḫosrau. Like Mīr Ḫūrd, he, too, was exiled to the Deccan where he died in 1328. He has been called 'the Sa'di of India,' a fitting surname, since he displays the same lucid simplicity of style as the great poet of Shiraz in his *ġazals* which are generally held together by a single conception. He had also to write some *qaṣīdas*, and composed a romantic *maṯnawī*, *'išqnāma*, based on a Hindu folktale —such adaptations of Indian material into Persian poetry are not infrequent in the subsequent centuries. Some critics hold that Ḥasan's sweet and unassuming style is superior to most of Amīr Ḫosrau's *ġazals* which, despite their musical elegance, are often slightly too cerebral.

---

71 K. A. Nizami, Malfūẓāt kī tārīḫī ahammiyat, Arshi Presentation Vol., Delhi 1965; further his tā'riḫ-i mašā'iḫ-i čišt, Delhi 1953, and Some Aspects (vd. note 61).

72 Lucknow 1302 h/1885; Ḥasan's kulliyāt ed. Mas'ud Ali Mahvi, Hyderabad 1352 h/1933; Marek/R 717f.; E 303.—Cf. M. J. Borah, The Life and Work of Amīr Hasan Dihlavi, JASB 1941.

73 Delhi 1302 h/1885; cf. Storey Nr. 1259 (the subsequent paragraphs in Storey contain much important material for this field).

74 maktūbāt Lucknow 1898; his ma'dan al-ma'ānī Bihar 1301/1884.

The poet Badr-i Čāč from Tashkent (d. 1346) found a home at Muḥammad ibn Tughluq's court, where he composed 30000 verses of *qaṣīda* in unusually difficult style, and a *Šāhnāma* of 20000 verses which is, like some of his panegyrics, an interesting historical source.[75] In comparison to his work, Muṭahhar Karā Dihlawī's panegyrics are simpler.[76]

The Sufi Ḍiyā'uddīn Naḫšabī (d. 1350) wrote about the education of mystical adepts and composed poetry in honour of the Prophet, but is mainly noted for his *Ṭūṭīnāma* 'The Book of the Parrot', after a Sanskrit parable.[77] This book, which has been imitated by Urdu poets and was translated into several Asian and European languages as well, shows a motif that is common in Indo-Muslim lore: the parrot, connected with Paradise because of its lovely green colour and excelling by virtue of its ability to speak, often appears to convey mystical or religious instruction—other examples may be found in Miḥrābī's still unpublished apologetic work *ḥuǧǧat al-Hind* (17. cty.) and also in some sacred texts of the Indian Ismailis.

At Firozshah Tughluq's court lived Mas'ūd Beg (d. 1397) who gave up his court position and devoted himself to a Sufi life, becoming renowned for talking intoxicated verses. Other mystics continued writing commentaries upon the classical works of Sufism. While the interest previously had centered mainly upon the teachings of al-Ġazzālī and Suhrawardi whose works had been partly translated into Persian, in the later 14th century Ibn 'Arabī's (d. 1240) influence became clearly visible in Indo-Muslim literature. Gīsūdarāz, the Čištī saint of Golconda, has played a decisive role in this development. We have mentioned him as the learned author of works in Arabic; he was likewise a prolific writer in Persian whose mystical poetry consists mainly of exuberant love-songs (*anīs al-'uššāq*, 'The intimate Friend of the Lovers'):

"Those who are intoxicated from the goblet of love
Are out of their senses due to the wine of *alastu* (the pre-eternal covenant between God and man, as mentioned in Sura 7/171);
Sometimes they strive for piety and ritual prayer,
Sometimes they drink wine and are idol-worshippers,
Whatever they saw on the tablet of Being,
They washed it off, except the image of the Beloved.
They have passed beyond Divine Throne and Footstool,
They sat down in the chamber of No-Where . . ."

He translated classical Arabic works into Persian and composed also the first mystical book in the Dakhni vernacular.[78]

---

[75] qaṣā'id, ed. Hadi Ali, Cawnpore 1845; Lucknow 1907; Marek/R 719.

[76] M. W. Mirza, Muṭahhar-i Karā, Oriental College Mag. 5/1935; M. Shirwani, qaṣā'id-i Muṭahhar-i Karā, Ma'ārif 8/1935.

[77] E 324f. gives its history and translation into various languages; W. Pertsch, Ueber Nachschabis Papageienbuch, ZDMG 21/1869; First English translation by M. Gerrans, London 1792; German translation by K. H. Iken, with explanations by J. Kosegarten, Leipzig 1822; G. Rosen (after the Turkish version) Leipzig 1858.

[78] dīvān anīs al-'uššāq, lith. s.d., s.l.; the mi'rāǧ al-'āšiqīn (Urdu) ed. Maulvi Abdul Haqq, Hyderabad 1927; cf. also note 15.

At approximately the same time, Muslim literature in Kashmir was strengthened by the arrival of 'Alī Hamadānī, the leading mystic of the Kubrāwīya order, who settled there and died in Swat in 1384.[79] This 'prince and dervish and counsellor of kings' not only composed Arabic writings, but also a large number of Persian works on Sufi technical terms, commentaries on Ibn 'Arabī's and Suhrawardī's books, and last but not least among the 170 books ascribed to him the *daḫīrat al-mulūk* 'Treasure of the Kings,' a 'mirror for princes' which gained wide fame. With Hamadānī and his disciples the literary Persian tradition had its real beginning in Kashmir:[80] Under Sultan Sikandar (1389–1418) and Zain al-'Abidīn (1420–70) Persian became widely accepted as the literary language. Under the Chak dynasty (1561–89) both religious and court poetry flourished. Among the poets, mention should be made of Ya'qūb Ġanā'ī Ṣarfī (d. 1591) who composed i.a. an imitation of Niẓāmī's *Ḫamsa* in which the *Iskandarnāme* is substituted by the *maġāzī an-nabī* 'The Prophet's Battles.' Sufi works and a commentary of Faiḍī's *sawāṭi' al-ilhām* flowed likewise from his pen. Under the later Mughals Kashmir became once more the favourite resort of kings and poets, so that almost every Mughal poet has written something about its natural beauties and the splendid buildings erected by the emperors.

It goes without saying that the historical literature continued in all parts of Muslim India.[81] As the main work on the Sayyid Dynasty of Delhi (1414–51) we may mention Yaḥyā ibn 'Abdallāh Sirhindī's *ta'rīḫ-i Mubārakšāhī*.[82] In the southern kingdoms, the rulers of Malwa—an important centre of Islamic culture—and Gujrat had their court historiographers as well.[83]

Persian culture was at that time widespread in the whole Subcontinent. It is said that Sultan Ghiyathuddīn of Bengal invited the poet Ḥāfiẓ of Shiraz (d. 1389) to visit his court. The mystical poetry of Ġalāluddīn Rūmī (d. 1273), the greatest Sufi poet in Persian tongue, was read wherever Muslims reached—even in distant Bengal to the extent that 'the holy Brahmin will recite the *Maṯnawī*.'[84] In that part of the Subcontinent, Ibrahim Qiwāmuddīn Fārūqī composed, in 1448, a Persian dictionary *farhang-i Ibrāhīmī* or *šarafnāma*, the latter title in honour of the saintly Šarafuddīn al-Manērī. Ibrāhīm followed the example of Badruddīn Muḥammad who, living in Malwa, had written his

[79] E 349f.; Storey p. 946 note 4; Tauer/R 427; cf. note 17.

[80] G. L. Tikku, Persian Poetry in Kashmir, Los Angeles 1971.

[81] Cf. Hameed ud-Din, The Sayyids, The Lodis, in: R. C. Majumdar, The Delhi Sultanate, Bombay ²1967.

[82] Cf. S. C. Misra, Muslim Communities in Gujrat, Bombay 1964;—ta'rīḫ-i Mubārakšāhī, ed. Calcutta 1931; transl. K. K. Basu, Baroda 1932.

[83] 'Alī b. Muḥammad Kirmānī, ma'āṯir-i Maḥmūdšāhī, a biography of Maḥmūd Khalǧi of Malwa (1436–69), unpublished, vd. Hameed ud-Din, l.c. p. 752;—Faḍlullāh ibn Zain ul-'Abidīn, ṭabāqāt-i Maḥmūdšāhī 1499 (Gujrat) and 'Abdulkarīm, ta'rīḫ-i Maḥmūdšāhī, a history of Gujrat up to 1484, both unpublished, cf. Hameed ud-Din, l.c. 759, 760.

[84] M. Enamul Haq, Muslim Bengali Literature, Karachi 1957, p. 42.

dictionary *'ādat al-fuḍalā'* 'Custom of the Virtuous' in 1419.[85] India was indeed to become 'the home of Persian lexicography'—during the late Lodi period (1451–1526) Maḥmūd Ḍiyā'uddīn's *farhang-i sikandarī* and Šaiḫ Muḥammad's *mu'ayyid al-fuḍalā'* 'Supporter of the Virtuous' were written in Delhi.

For a new impetus in the study of Persian is visible during the reign of Sikandar Lōdī (1479–1517) who, as a mediocre poet, used the pen-name Gulruḫī.[86] His verses were corrected by Ǧamālī Kanbōh (d. 1535), the author of both lyrics and romantic *maṯnawīs* (like *Mihr u Māh* 'Sun and Moon') and also of hagiographical literature (*siyar al-'ārifīn* about Čišti saints).[87] Ǧamālī had widely travelled and had spent some time in Herat, where he became friendly with Ǧāmī and Ḥusain Wā'iẓ Kāšifī, the author of the *anwār-i suhailī*, 'Lights of Canopus,' a collection of tales based on *Kalilah wa Dimna* which was, later, reworked in India by Abū'l-Faḍl so that the originally Indian fables eventually returned to their homeland. The style of both Ǧāmī and Ḥusain Wā'iẓ was to become most influential in Indo-Persian poetry from ca. 1500 onwards. Ǧamālī's own poetry is attractive and informative, often tinged with Sufi ideals. One of his lighter poems which has become almost proverbial excels by its charming simplicity and the use of exclusively diminutive nouns:

"A little reed-mat of two little yards and a little sheep-skin,
A little heart filled with pain of a little friend,
A little *lungi* below, a little *lungi* above,
Neither grief about a thief, nor grief about household-goods—
That much is enough for Ǧamālī,
The intoxicated, care-free lover."

Also during this period books on Indian medicine *(ma'dan-i šifā'-yi Sikandaršāhī)*[88] and on music were composed under the auspices and with the participation of Miān Bhawan, Sikandar Lōdī's highly accomplished minister (executed 1512). One of the most interesting trends during the Lōdī period is the increasing participation of Hindus in Persian literature; henceforward they utilized every Persian literary genre, including the praise of the Prophet.[89] The most reliable Persian history of this period was written only in the mid 16th century by Muštāqī, related to many important figures of the Lōdī court.[90]

The heyday of Persian literature coincides with the Mughal rule.[91] H. Ethé

---

[85] About Persian lexicography in India cf. Tauer/R 430ff.

[86] Hameed ud-Din, Indian Culture in the late Sultanate Period, East and West NS 12/1, 1961.

[87] siyar ul-'ārifīn Delhi 1311 h/1893; Mihr u Māh, Panjab University Library; E 249; Storey Nr. 1280; MM 790.

[88] Tauer/R 475.

[89] Dr. Syed Abdullah, adabiyat-i fārsī meñ hindūoñ kā ḥiṣṣa, Delhi 1942.

[90] Best known is Aḥmad Yādgār, ta'rīḫ-i salāṭīn-i Lōdī wa Sūrī, or: ta'rīḫ-i Šāhī ed. Hidayat Husain, Calcutta 1939; cf. MM 167; Storey p. 516, 1312; according to Dr. Hameed ud-Din, the still unpublished wāqi'āt-i Muštāqī (1491–1582) is more trustworthy; MM 1338; Storey p. 513.

[91] S. R. Sharma, A Bibliography of Mughal India, Bombay s.d.; M. A. Ghani,

has rightly described this period as the 'Indian summer of Persian poetry,' for the colourful imagery of the later Persian poets who migrated, one by one, to the generous rulers of the Subcontinent can scarcely be surpassed; it ended in the autumnal hopelessness of bizarre poetical expressions.

However, the beginning of the Mughal period is marked by a work not in Persian but in Turkish, a language which must have been widely spoken in the Subcontinent, since most of the Muslim conquerors hailed from Central Asia, and the military aristocracy was Turkish to such an extent, that 'Turk' and 'Muslim' became equivalents in some Indian vernaculars. Already in the earliest Persian poetry, 'Turk' means usually the white, beautiful though cruel, and courageous beloved, the 'Hindu' usually being equated with the ugly black infidel slave. This imagery, so common in Persian literature, was adopted in India as well in many a poem: Amīr Ḫosrau has praised his Turkish beloved whose 'lowly Hindu' = 'slave' he wanted to become. Turkish remained a favourite language in the feudal classes, and dictionaries of Turkish were composed up to the late 18th century in India. Even Ġālib, in the 19th century, still boasts of his Turkish descent. That Turkish was known not only in the centres of the Mughal Empire but also in the provinces is seen from some works composed by writers in Sind: Faḫrī Harawī,[92] the well-known translator of Mīr 'Alī Šīr Nawā'i's *maǧālis an-nafā'is* from Turki into Persian, had left Herat when the Uzbegs overrun Afghanistan, settling, like his compatriote Ǧihāngīr Hāšimī (author of a mystical *maṯnawī*, d. 1539)[93] in Thatta. Faḫrī's *rauḍat as-salāṭīn* contains a considerable number of Turkish verses composed by Turkish rulers of Central Asia and Iran. Since both dynasties which ruled Sind after the fall of the Summa, i.e. the Arghuns and the Tarkhans, were of Turkish extraction, their rulers must have been able to enjoy Faḫrī's book.

The main work of Turkish literature in the Subcontinent, and one of the most fascinating books in the whole of Islamic literature, is the autobiography of Bābur who after his victory over Ibrāhīm Lōdī in Panipat 1526 laid the foundations of the Mughal Empire that was to attract the admiration of neighbouring countries and, later, even of Europe where the poets' eyes turned 'to Agra and Lahore of Great Moghul.' The *Bāburnāme*, or *tuzuk-i Bāburī*,[94]

A History of Persian Language and Literature at the Mughal Court, I–III, Allahabad 1929–30, repr. 1972; Hadi Hasan, Mughal Poetry: its cultural and historical value, Madras 1951.

[92] rauḍat as-salāṭīn wa ǧawāhir al-'aǧā'ib, ed. H. Rashdi, Hyderabad/Sind 1968; MM 442; Storey Nr. 1094, 1099; cf. E 213, 244.

[93] maṯnawī maẓhar ul-āṯār, ed. H. Rashdi, Karachi 1957; MM 622.

[94] Storey p. 529ff. gives a survey of the complete literature about the Bāburnāme. First English translation, from the Persian by J. Leyden and W. Erskine, London 1826; rev. Sir Lucas King, Oxford 1921; ed. and transl. by A. S. Beveridge, London 1921; the Dīvān was edited by Denison Ross, JRAS Bengal 1910, A. Samoilovich, Petrograd 1917, and F. Köprülü in Milli tetebbüler mecmuasi, Istanbul 1925ff. (vol. II, III, V, incomplete). His work on metrics is still in manuscript (Bibl. Nat. Paris, Suppl. Turc 1308). A beautiful edition of the finest illustrations of

is written in fresh and unsophisticated Čaġatay Turkish; it was translated into Persian thrice, once during the emperor's lifetime by Zainuddīn Ḫwāfī (d. 1533), then under Akbar by the Khānkhānān 'Abdurraḥīm.[95] Babur, born of a family in which poetical talent and literary taste were hereditary, was not only a brilliant prosewriter whose keen observations and poignant remarks about every aspect of life make his autobiography lively and enjoyable, but also a fairly good poet in both Turkish and Persian. He even composed a Turkish work on the art of metrics and rhetorics and versified some rather dull religious treatises.[96] A good example of his style is the description of the army's marching towards Kabul in winter 1506–7, when Babur was 23 years old:

> "Qasim Bey, by saying 'That way is long, let's go this way!' showed much lack of experience, but we went this way. There was a Pashai guide, called Pir Sultan. Be it due to his age, or to excitement, or because of the large amount of snow—he lost his way and could not bring us any further. Since we had taken this way due to Qasim Bey's obstinacy, Qasim Bey took it as a matter of honour, and he and his sons dug up the snow and, opening the road, went ahead. One day there was unusually much snow. We did no know our way either. A few times we tried, but we could not walk. Since we found no escape, we turned and went down to a place with trees. We decided that 70 to 80 good young boys should return following our footsteps and should take one of the Hazaras who spent the winter in the depth of the valley and bring him here so that he might be our guide. Until the going party came back, we stayed there three or four days. Those who had gone did not bring a man who could act as a good guide. Trusting in God, we put Sultan Pashai in front of us, and since we did not find the road we went once more the way we had come. During these few days we suffered extraordinary adversities and perturbations. During my whole life I have rarely suffered that much. During that period I said this *maṭla'* (first verse of a *ġazal*):
> Has there remained any tyranny and cruelty of the world which I did not see?
> Has there remained any pain and affliction that my sick heart did not taste?"

Babur's poetical talent was inherited by his children, one of whom, Kāmrān Mīrzā, wrote in Turkish,[97] whereas the others, including his daughter Gulbadan, choose Persian for their literary activities—Gulbadan's *Humāyūnnāma*[98] is a good account of the late days of Babur and the times after his death, as seen through the eyes of an intelligent lady of the royal household. The literary

---

the Baburname ms. preserved in the British Museum was published in Tashkent 1969. The two other illustrated mss. are in New Delhi and Moscow.

[95] Zainuddīn Khwāfī Wafā'ī MM 1845; a translation by Mīrzā Pāyanda Ḥasan MM 1072, 1227; Khānkhānān's translation lith. Bombay 1308 h/1890. Cf. E 361.

[96] About Babur as an author cf. F. Teufel, Bābur und Abū Fażl, ZDMG 38/1883; A. Schimmel, Bābur Padishah, the Poet, with an account of the poetical talent in his family, IC 1960. Among his talented relatives connected with Indian history mention must be made of Mīrzā Ḥaidar Dūghlāt, tā'rīḫ-i rašīdī, transl. E. Denison Ross and N. Elias, London 1898; cf. E 359; Storey 273ff.; MM 1066.

[97] Dīvān, ed. Mahfuzul Haq, A'zamgarh 1929; Alam Khan, Mirza Kamran, Aligarh 1964; MM 849.

[98] Humāyūnnāme, History of Humayun, transl. A. S. Beveridge, London 1902; ed. Lucknow 1925, Tashkent 1959; MM 550; Storey p. 538.

tradition of the Mughal house was continued by Humāyūn,[99] Akbar (who, though scarcely writing poetry himself, encouraged literary life to a hitherto unknown extent) and Jihāngīr. The latter's autobiography, *tuzuk-i ǧihāngīrī*,—extant in three versions—gives a lively picture of his rather gay life devoted to pleasure, hunting, and collecting jewels and other precious items like miniatures.[100] Two of the best representatives of the literary talent of the Mughal dynasty are the unlucky prince Dārā Shikōh and his sister Jihānārā. Dārā's younger brother, the later ruler 'Ālamgīr Aurangzeb, also possessed an excellent literary style;[101] his daughter, Zēb un-Nisā', is credited with touching Persian verses. Even the politically weak rulers of the 18th and 19th centuries were at least good poets, notably Shah 'Alam II Aftāb who, like his son Sulaimān Shikōh (exiled in Lucknow) took to Urdu; and the last Mughal ruler, Bahādur Shah Ẓafar, who is one of the finest lyrical poets in Urdu language.

As to the Turkish tradition inaugurated by Babur, one may assume that at the Sindhi court some poets besides Faḫrī wrote, at least in part, in Turkish. A veritable master of this language was Bairam Khān (d. 1561) from the Aqqoyunlu Turcomans, Babur's and Humayun's faithful generallissimo who was mainly responsible for Akbar's accession to the throne.[102] Whereas Bairam Khān was more expressive in his Turkish poetry than in his rather conventional Persian verses, his son Khānkhānān 'Abdurraḥīm (1556–1626) excelled in both these languages as well as in Hindi.[103] His military achievements are most impressive: the conquest of Ahmedabad in Gujrat 1576 and a repeated victory in 1584, the successful wresting of Sind from the Tarkhans and its annexation to the Mughal Empire in 1591 and a long series of campaigns in the Deccan. Yet all of these activities did neither prevent him from writing tender verses in three languages, nor from giving patronage to poets, musicians, and painters from all over the Muslim world. 'He spent most of his time in the company of perfect and virtuous people, and poets and elegant men were during his government prosperous and without sorrows,' says 'Abdulbāqī Nihāwandī in

---

[99] Dīvān, ed. Hadi Hasan, IC 1951; MM 654; cf. Ghani, Persian Language vol. II. Other historical works dealing with Humāyūn: Gauhar Aftābǧī, taḏkirat al-wāqi'āt, defective transl. C. Stewart, London 1832; Urdu transl. by Moinul Haqq, Karachi 1955; MM 806; Storey p. 536; cf. further Bāyezīd, ta'rīḫ-i Humāyūn, ed. M. Hidayat Husain, Calcutta 1941; MM 334; Storey p. 538, 1313.

[100] tuzuk-i Jihāngīrī, 2. rev. ed. Sir Sayyid Ahmad Khan, Aligarh 1864; Lucknow 1914; transl. by Rogers and H. Beveridge, London 1909–14; the so-called 'Garbled memoirs,' ed. Calcutta 1904, had been transl. by D. Price, Calcutta 1829. Storey Nr. 720; MM 772. Urdu transl. by I. H. Quddusi, Lahore 1970.

[101] About his literary activites E 342f.; MM 283; ruqa'āt-i 'Ālamgīrī ed. Lucknow 1260 h/1844; ed. Sayyid N. A. Nadwi, Azamgarh 1930, and different editions. English transl. by D. H. Billimoria, Bombay 1908.

[102] Bayram Khan, The Persian and Turki Divans, ed. Denison Ross, Calcutta 1910; ed. M. Sabir and H. Rashdi, Karachi 1971; MM 377.

[103] Cf. Ghani III 220ff.; MM 62, 1518; Vanshiddar, Abdur Raḥīm and his Hindi poetry, IC 1950.

the *ma'āṯir-i raḥīmī.*[104] This work dwells in detail upon Khānkhānān's political and cultural role and shows that he was indeed one of the key figures in the heydays of the Mughal Empire. 31 religious leaders, 104 poets and 49 artists lived in his entourage. Without his deep love for fine arts and his boundless generosity the stream of poets and artists who came from Iran to seek their fortune in India would surely not have been so large.

In fact, the immigration of Persian artists almost coincides with the beginning of Mughal rule. Humāyūn, Bābur's son, had to seek shelter at the court of the Safawid Shah of Iran, Tahmasp; upon his return, he brought a number of poets and artists with him to India. The spiritual climate of Safawid Iran was not very congenial for poets, particularly for those with mystical inclinations. As one of them says:

> There exist not in Persia the means of acquiring perfection:
> Henna does not develop its colour until it comes to India.[105]

Badā'ūnī mentions some 170 Persian poets, 59 of them living at the court, who flourished during Akbar's reign of nearly half a century (1556–1605). Treatises about fine arts, or biographies of calligraphers and miniaturists are therefore not rare in this period. One of the strangest figures among the poets is Maulānā Qāsim Kāhī[106] from Central Asia who panegyrized Humāyūn in Kabul and died in Agra in 1580, allegedly at the age of 120. The few verses which have been preserved from his prolific output show a most elegant use of witty imagery.

In 1582, Persian was made, by decree, the official government language, and Akbar displayed a special interest in the compilation of dictionaries; the most important one was completed by its author Ǧamāluddīn Ḥusain Inǧū only in 1623 and therefore called *farhang-i ǧihāngīrī.*[107] It may be noted at random that the famous humorist at Akbar's court, Mollā Dō Piyāze, composed his 'dictionary' as a parody on Arabic dictionaries.[108]

During early Mughal days, the activity of the mystics showed itself in practical life and in writing; the towering figure of 'Abdulquddūs al-Gangōhī (d. 1538), a prolific writer in Arabic and Persian, deserves special mention.[109] Strictly obedient to the Muslim law, he was also a follower of the theories of *waḥdat al-wuǧūd*, the so-called 'pantheistic' trend in Sufism, a combination

---

[104] Ed. M. Hidayat Husain, Calcutta 1910–31; MM 13; Storey p. 553.

[105] E. G. Browne, A Literary History of Persian in Modern Times (Vol. IV), Cambridge repr. 1953, p. 166 where other examples are given; cf. E § 43 about Indo-Persian poets.

[106] Hadi Hasan, Qāsim Kāhī, his Life, Time, and Works, IC 1953; Ghani II 55f.; MM 831; Marek/R 723.

[107] Tauer/R 431; MM 788; cf. also the farhang-i Surūrī, composed in 1599, printed Tabriz 1844: MM 1760.

[108] MM 434, 1306.

[109] I. H. Quddusi, Šaiḫ 'Abdul Quddūs Gangōhī aur unkī ta'līmāt, Karachi 1961; cf. Storey Nr. 1279; MM 58.

often found in later Sufism. His grandson 'Abdunnabī, for a time chief justice of the Empire, likewise excelled as author of some Arabic theological works; having aroused Akbar's aversion he was murdered in prison in 1582.[110]

The literature written during Akbar's time was largely influenced by the interest the ruler himself took in the translation of Sanskrit works into Persian—an attempt, albeit not a very successful one, to promote the understanding between the representatives of the two major religious and social systems of his empire.[111] The Mahābhārata was rendered into Persian as *razmnāma*. We find also a *ta'rīḫ-i Krišnağī*, and a translation of the *Yoga Vasišta* as well as translations of books on Indian music. The *Singhasan battīsī*, '32 Throne Stories,' were adapted first under Akbar (1574), and translated anew under each of the following three emperors. Hindu themes, though previously used on occasion in Persian poetry, became more fashionable; the best example being Nau'ī's (d. 1610) tragic epic *sūz u gudāz* 'Burning and Melting' which tells the story of a young woman who committed *satī* during Akbar's reign. This poem was also illustrated several times.[112]

Among the translators of scholarly and religious books was the pious and ingenious Mollā 'Abdulqādir Badā'ūnī. He viewed his activities as translator as a veritable spiritual punishment, as we see from his words written upon the completion of his translation of Vālmīki's *Ramāyaṇa* after 1580:

> I seek God's protection from the cursed writing which is as wretched as the parchment of my life. The reproduction of infidelity does not mean infidelity. I utter word in refutation of infidelity, for I fear lest this book written at the order of the Emperor entirely might bear the print of hatred.

This feeling of hatred against the rendering of pagan stories and polytheistic religious works (Badā'ūnī also worked on the *Atharvaveda*) on the part of pious Muslim scholars was even more openly expressed in Badā'ūnī's historical work, the *muntaḫab at-tawārīḫ*,[113] based upon Ḫʷağā Niẓāmuddīn Aḥmad's *ṭabaqāt-i Akbarī*, 1593, the earliest of the general histories exclusively devoted to India.[114]

---

[110] GAL S II 602; ZA IV 17; MM 50.

[111] About translations from the Sanscrit cf. E 352–55; Marek/R 724.

[112] English Version by MIRZA Y. DAWUD and DR. A. K. COOMARASWAMY, London 1912. Printed at the end of Vol. 1 of Akbarnāme, Lucknow 1284 h/1867; E 254; MM 1388. Some beautifully illustrated mss. of the poem are found i.a. in the Chester Beatty Library Nr. 268, 269, and Bibl. Nationale, Paris, Suppl. Pers. 769. For the problem of Indian influences cf. S. A. ABIDI, Indian Elements in Indo-Persian Literature, Delhi 1969. For a similar Hindu topic cf. S. A. H. ABIDI, The Story of Padmavat in Indo-Persian Literature, Indo-Iranica XV 2, 1963.

[113] Ed. W. N. LEES, Maulwi Kabiruddin and Maulwi Ahmad Ali, Calcutta 1864–69; transl. Vol. 1 by G. RANKING, Vol. II by W. H. LOWE, Vol. III by T. W. HAIG, Calcutta 1884–1925. Storey p. 438ff.; MM 53 a survey of all his extant works. Badā'ūnī was also one of the contributors to the ta'rīḫ-i alfī of Mollā Aḥmad Tattawī, cf. E 356; Storey p. 118f.; MM 166.

[114] Niẓāmuddīn Aḥmad Baḫšī, ṭabaqāt-i Akbarī, ed. B. DE and MAULWI HIDAYAT HUSAIN, Calcutta 1913–40, transl. B. De and B. PRASHAD, Calcutta 1927ff.; Storey p. 433f.; MM 1413.

In this book Badā'ūnī's accumulated antipathy against the Emperor's actions is reflected in sometimes surprising details. For a balanced picture of the period, one must read Badā'ūnī's chronicle together with the official history of Akbar's court, Abū'l-Faḍl's *Akbarnāma* (the third part of which, *āyin-i Akbarī*, is indeed the most interesting positive description of Mughal life).[115]

Abū'l-Faḍl and his elder brother Faiḍī were the main scapegoats of the orthodox in their criticism of Akbar's regime. These two accomplished and learned men, sons of Šaiḫ Muḥammad Nāgōrī[116] and thus hailing from a family connected with the chiliastic movement of the Mahdī of Jawnpur (d. 1505), are said to have induced the emperor to invent the *dīn-i ilāhī*, a religion of sheer eclecticism. Abū'l-Faḍl 'Allāmī drafted the decree which enabled Akbar to settle theological arguments. He was a versatile scholar who i. a. translated the Bhagavadgītā and the Bible, wrote a new recension of Ḥusain Wā'iẓ Kāšifī's *anwār-i suhailī* under the title *'iyār-i dāniš* 'Criterion of Knowledge' (1588) and composed some collections of official letters.[117] His assassination in 1602 at the instigation of Prince Salīm (later Jihāngīr) while on assignment in the Deccan was one of the actions for which Akbar never forgave his heir apparent.

Abū'l-Faḍl's elder brother Faiḍī, mentioned already as the author of a commentary of the Quran in undotted letters, wrote much lyrical and mystical poetry as well as a Persian *Ḫamsa*;[118] one part of which deals with the famous Sanskrit story of Nala and Damayantī *(Nāl Daman)*. He became poet laureate *(malik as-šu'arā')* of Akbar, an office recently established by the emperor; its first representative being Ġazālī Mašhadī (d. 1572).[119] The general aversion against Faiḍī is understood from one of the unfriendly chronograms concerning his death: *būd Faiḍī mulḥidī*—1104/1595 'Faiḍi was a heretic.' Verses like this make the aversion of the orthodox understandable:

"Come, so that we may turn our faces towards the arch of light,
We lay the foundation of a new Ka'ba with the stone from Mount Sinai;
The four walls of the Ka'ba broke, and the foundation of the qibla gave way,
Anew we lay the foundation of a faultless structure."

---

[115] Ed. Cawnpore 1881–83, Calcutta 1873–1886, ²1953; transl. by H. BEVERIDGE, Calcutta 1897–1939. A beautiful illustrated copy of the Akbarname is preserved in the Victoria and Albert Museum, London (cf. S. C. WELSH, The Art of Mughal India, New York 1963 p. 27). A'īn-i Akbarī, vol. I–III, ed. H. BLOCHMANN, Calcutta 1867–77, 1939; transl. H. BLOCHMANN and H. S. JARETT, 1868–94; rev. D. C. PHILLOTH, Calcutta 1939–40; cf. Ghani III 233; Storey Nr. 709; MM 99; Tauer/R 449.

[116] About him ZA I 10.

[117] 'iyār-i dāniš printed Cawnpore 1879, Lucknow 1892; cf. E 327–8 about the development of this kind of literature, and also R 313. His letters have been printed several times as maktūbāt-i Abū'l-Faḍl, maktūbāt-i 'Allāmī, or mukātabat-i 'Allāmī.

[118] E 308; MM 468; R 299; Ghani III 39; cf. note 33. Nāl Daman printed Lucknow 1877, 1930.

[119] E 298; MM 492.

"The lover, from whose unhappy life grief does not depart,
Till life is in him, the warmth and convulsions continue;
A lover has the property of quicksilver,
Until he is dead, his restlessness does not leave him."
(Ghani III 49, 56).

One of the favourite topics of literary criticism in the Persian speaking world was the comparison between Faiḍī and his contemporary 'Urfī, the poet from Shiraz who reached Ahmadnagar in 1585 at the age of 29; he joined the Khānkhānān and eventually Akbar; in 1591, he died prematurely. The Turkish writer Ẓiya Pasha (d. 1879) says in his *ḫarābāt*:

> Faiḍī and 'Urfi run neck and neck, they are the leaders of later times. In Faiḍī is eloquence and freshness, in 'Urfī sweetness and fluency. In Faiḍī is fiery exhortation while 'Urfī is strong in elegies. But if preeminence be sought, excellence still remains with Faiḍī.

Today we would scarcely agree with this statement which is similar to that of H. Ethé. The majestic *qaṣīdas* of 'Urfī reveal more of his personal problems, and his alleged pride and haughtiness may well be the expression of a most sensitive mind. His style is much more pathetic than that of the cooler and more intellectual Faiḍī.[120] Some of his *qaṣīdas*—upon which his fame mainly rests—belong to the greatest poems of the Persian language—and this cannot be said about Faiḍī's brilliant verses, technically impeccable as they may be. Some of 'Urfī's *ġazals* and quatrains are also memorable for their dark beauty, filled with 'new and original combinations of words, fine metaphors and a congruity of topics' (Shibli).

"What is the habit of lovers? To hold the assemblies of sorrow,
To form a circle of mourning, and to lament for the coming woes,
On the shore of the ocean of grief to produce the wave of delight,
To keep ready the army of pain on the battlefield of the heart,
To stitch the praises of pain and grief on the lip of the heart,
To keep the city of the heart and the garden of life devoted to suffering . . ."
(Ghani III 116).

These lines show the difference between 'Urfī and Fayḍī, whose description of the lover we just quoted. The darkness of 'Urfī's poetry is well understood from the following, very typical, lines from a *ġazal*:

"Come, O Pain, for I have the wish to flee from rest,
The wish to be joined with grief, to be cut off from joy!
Come, O Love, and make me the ignominious one of the world,
For I have the wish to hear a few good advices from those without pain! . . .
Come, O Fortune, and provoke a festive approximation for the sake of my killing,
Since I have the wish to see my soul slaughtered by that glance! . . .
Come, O Death, and befriend me! for without Him, how long can I stand it?
I wallowed in blood—now, I have the wish to rest."

---

[120] E 308, where four Persian and five Turkish commentaries are mentioned; MM 1812; R 299; Ghani III 103ff.; E. G. Browne, l.c. 242 (with the quotation from Żiyā Pasha). 'Urfī's *qaṣā'id* were printed Lahore 1924, and often with commentaries; ed. Kulliyāt, Teheran, ca. 1961.

'Urfī's complicated style—which is still simple compared to that of the subsequent generations—has always attracted commentators; he also exerted considerable influence on Ottoman poetry from the 17th century onwards.

'Urfī is regarded as one of the first masters of the *sabk-i hindī*, the Indian style which became notorious for its increasing complexity during the 17th century.[121] We find the first traces of this style as early as in Amīr Ḫosrau's verses, and Ǧāmī's artistic lyrics certainly contributed to its formation. The later development of this literary style is highly interesting: the poets, most of them from Iran, felt the need for expressing traditional ideas in a far more sophisticated fashion than previously. Since the topics remained, by and large, the same, and the literary forms were fixed once for all the style had to be elaborated. The former harmony between the different parts of an image or a trope was often broken up, and the disrupted parts of a simile put together in a new and unexpected way. The poets developed a predilection for the use of the infinitive (even in the plural!) and of abstract nouns. The language was enriched with words from colloquial Persian or loanwords from Hindi. In addition to breaking and rearranging the inherited images, the poets expanded their imagery with a number of new similes taken from daily life at the Mughal court and from contemporary events: The *firangī*, the European, is mentioned more often; the eyeglasses (introduced, according to the witness of miniatures, towards the end of the 16th century) provided an oft-used image, as did the hour-glass which is, itself, seen for the first time on miniatures of the Jihangir period.[122] Fine arts and poetry can often be used to explain each other; poetry can be utilized to an unusual degree as a source of knowledge of everyday life, provided the reader has enough patience to solve all the riddles posed by the convoluted style. Descriptive poetry becomes more common; proverbial sayings are not infrequently introduced into the second hemistich of a verse. In many cases, the language loses its sweet and easy flow as difficult metres and far-fetched rhymes are applied to demonstrate the technical perfection of the artists, or rather artisans.

This style can produce most interesting results in the hands of a true poet who may be able truly to impress the reader by verses in which deep melancholia is often blended with strong spiritual restlessness. The situation of the slowly decaying Mughal Empire is reflected in the mood of many of these 17th century poets in whose verses the frequent use of words like 'breaking,' 'smoke,' 'getting burnt,' 'blister,' 'footprint,' 'shifting sand-dune,' etc. is a characteristic feature. Naẓīrī (d. 1612), one of the early representatives of the *sabk-i hindī*,

[121] Cf. R 295ff.; A. Bausani, Contributo a una definizione del 'stilo indiano' della poesie persiane (Ann. Ist. Univ. Orient. Napoli, NS VII, 1958); the same, Storia delle letterature dell Pakistan, Milano 1959 (a book which is relevant for the whole complex of Indo-Muslim poetry). W. Heinz, Der indische Stil in der persischen Dichtung, ZDMG, Suppl. I 2, Wiesbaden 1969.

[122] Cf. R. Ettinghausen, Paintings of the Sultans and Emperors of India, New Delhi, s.d., pl. 14.

says: 'Seek a far meaning and bring a far-fetched word,' thus highlighting the character of his own and his colleagues' art.

Naẓīrī—considered the most pious of the Mughal poets—had come from Nishapur and went to Agra where 'Abdurraḥīm Khānkhānān became his maecenas;[123] not less than ten *qaṣīdas* of his in honour of his patron are listed in the *ma'āṯir-i raḥīmī*. His style has influenced later poets considerably; even Iqbal has quoted him and written a *naẓīra* to one of his poems.

Another famous master of elegant Indian style is Nūruddīn Muḥammad Ẓuhūrī (d. 1615), born in Khorassan.[124] He spent the greater part of his life not at the Mughal court but with the 'Adilshāhīs in Bijapur where the ruler, Ibrāhīm 'Adilshāh II (1580–1626) was a poet in his own right (writing, however, mainly in Dakhni). Ẓuhūrī's *ruq'āt* contain anecdotes and stories in extremely flowery rhymed prose. An essay written as introduction to a Dakhni book on music composed by his patron Ibrahim abounds in musical imagery. Thus he says in his *Gulzār-i Ibrāhīm* when describing the virtues of his patron and dwelling upon the ninth virtue, that of acquiring excellences and perfection:

"In estimating his bright genius the lofty sky is a cripple; and in contrast with his meditation and sound judgment, the deep sea is a tiny wave. With the miracle of his David-like songs he softens the iron-hearts into wax; and with the freshness of his *barbūd*-like notes, he picks away the dryness from off the brain of the pious (i.e., even pious people, who have no passion for music, are amused with his charming melodies). In the garden of music, the body of Venus, with the flower of acknowledgment of his pupilship, is decorating her head (i.e., Venus considers it an honour to acknowledge herself as his pupil in the art of music); and on the page of his writing the cipher of Jupiter has its position exalted by the cipher of his testing pen (i.e. just as each cipher placed after another increases the value tenfold, so his cipher placed with that of Jupiter heightens its position) . . ."

And he closes his writing with a *maṯnawī* in which he sings the greatness of Ibrahim:

"The Deccan is the home of mirth and happiness; the lip is thrown into a foreign land by the talk of one's native country. It is not strange that the morn of the day of joyous meeting of the happy lovers with their beloveds may fell ashamed before the evening of a homeless traveller (entering the King's city). Exquisite tunes are poured forth from his musical instrument; ay, the king is the comforter of the stranger . . .
. . . The story is ended, may the garden of his face be an object of envy for the rose-garden of Abraham!" (Ghani III 381, 388, 389).

Ẓuhūrī's fame rests mainly with his *sāqīnāma* in which he describes the joyful life at the court in Bijapur in delightful short verses, using the so-called 'heroic

[123] Dīvān, ed. T. Muṣaffā, Teheran 1340 s.; MM 1395; Ghani III 66ff.; for him and the following poets cf. R 301, Marek/R 723ff.; E. G. Browne, l.c. 250ff.; M. L. Rahman, Persian Literature during the time of Jahangir and Shah Jehan, Baroda 1970.

[124] E 309, 336; MM 1931; Marek/R 724f.; Ghani II 181ff.; Sih naṯr-i Ẓuhūrī Lucknow 1259 h/1843, ed. and transl. in Ghani III 307–467. About Ẓuhūrī's father-in-law Malik Qummī, another successful poet cf. MM 1018. Ibrahim Adilshah's nawras ed. Nazir Ahmad, Lucknow 1955.

metre' *mutaqārib*, a metre often used in India for descriptive lyrical poetry and *ġazals* (That is also true for Urdu poetry). Ẓuhūrī's *sāqīnāma* is a worthy match for the colourful miniatures which were painted during those years at the 'Ādilshāhī court where poets like Atašī, the author of an *'ādilnāma*,[125] and Mīr Muḥammad Hāšim Sanǧar (d. 1622) added to its splendour.[126]

In Delhi, where Jihāngīr and his capable queen Nūr Jihān encouraged poets and poetry, Ṭālib-i Āmulī (d. 1626) became poet laureate in 1619. Ṭālib was a highly intellectual poet who mastered many sciences at an early age, before coming to India.[127] He wrote every kind of poetry, including the epical chronicle *ǧihāngīrnāma*. His line about his emigration has become almost proverbial:

> Nobody ever brought a Hindu to India—
> Thus you had better leave your 'black fortune' (e.g. misfortune) in Iran—

the Hindu as symbol for 'black' could easily serve as a cypher for 'misfortune.' Indeed, Ṭālib made his fortune at the Mughal court, and many of his verses have been imitated by later writers even though they appeal but little to modern European taste.

Ṭālib's compatriote, Muḥammad Ṣūfī Māzandarānī reached India some time before him; he lived in Ahmadabad and died on his way to Jihāngīr's court in 1625; his main fame rests upon his poetic anthology *butḫāna* 'Idol temple.'[128]

Under Jihāngīr's successor Shāh Jihān the stream of writers from Iran continued; of these Ḥāǧǧī Muḥammad Ǧān Qudsī from Mashhad (d. 1656 in Kashmir) is worth mentioning. His range of complicated poetical effusions spans from a famous eulogy of the Prophet to wine-poetry and to a *ẓafarnāma-yi šāhǧihānī*, an epic celebrating the victories of his patron.[129]

Quite different from Qudsī's highly sophisticated and rather cerebral verses are most of the poems of Abū'l-Barakāt Munir Lāhōrī (1609–1645).[130] From Lahore which had become once more a centre of intellectual life thanks to Jihāngīr, Munīr travelled extensively, and one of his journeys resulted in a charming *maṯnawī* on Bengal. His poetry was simpler than that of his contemporaries and hence was less in vogue, although his *dīvān* is said to have contained 100000 verses. Famous is his epistolographic work; he composed also a commentary to 'Urfī's *qaṣīdas*—such commentaries were quite often composed by learned poets of the period.

Munīr was also a man of his time in writing a *taḏkira* of poets, for the 17th

---

125 Written 1627, E 238; MM 281.

126 E 308; MM 1644.

127 E 309; MM 1269 and 1779; Marek/R 725f.; Zitat Browne l.c. IV 255. Kulliyāt, ed. Ṭahirī Šihāb, Teheran 1346 š.; Khawāja 'Abd-ar-Rashīd, taḏkira-yi Ṭālib-i Āmulī, Karachi 1965.

128 MM 1265; Storey Nr. 1112.

129 MM 1496; Storey Nr. 727; Marek/R 727; S. A. Abidi, Life and Poetry of Qudsi Mashhadi, IC 1964. About more epical works in honour of Shahjihan and his sons cf. E 238.

130 MM 1318; about his epistolography E 341.

century was the time when *hommes-de-lettres* began to collect every conceivable bit of information about classical and contemporary poets and compiled biographical dictionaries. One of those famous for their *tadkira*'s is the prolific Taqī Auḥadī (d. 1630) who came to India in 1606.[131] His production includes *qaṣīdas* and *maṭnawīs* as well as a Persian dictionary *(surma-yi sulaimānī)* and a *tadkira* called *'arafāt al-'āšiqīn* 'The mountain Arafat of the Lovers,' a title which gives the date of its completion, i.e. 1024/1615. The book deals with 3168 Persian poets, and one of Taqī's numerous versions of this compilation, an extract called *ka'ba-yi 'irfān* 'The Ka'ba of Gnosis' was often used by later writers. Taqī's contemporary, 'Abdunnabī Qazwīnī, who reached Agra in 1609 at the age of 22, became a librarian and visited Kashmir and Bihar.[132] His collection *maiḫāna* 'The Tavern' contains the most famous *sāqīnāmas* he knew. 'Abdunnabī was, at the same time, an authority on the *qiṣṣa-yi Ḥamza*, the popular tale about the heroic deeds of Amir Ḥamza, the Prophet's uncle, that has been told and retold through the centuries in Muslim India and which was marvellously illustrated during Akbar's days.[133]

Another specialist on poets' biographies was Amīn Rāzī, a first cousin of Shāh Jihān's father-in-law I'timād ad-daula. He had compiled, in 1594, the *haft iqlīm* 'Seven Climata,' a work dealing with about 1560 poets, saints and scholars arranged according to their towns and countries, so that not only the historian of literature but the geographer as well can draw upon it.[134]

In the first years of Shāh Jihān's reign, Mirza Muḥammad 'Alī Ṣā'ib (1607–77) visited India. He stayed there for only six years, yet long enough considerably to influence the literary circles, for he was one of the outstanding masters of poignant diction, sometimes satirical, sometimes witty, sometimes melancholy, but always truly poetic.[135] Later Indo-Muslim poets have often drawn inspiration from his verses.—One of Ṣā'ib's friends was Abū Ṭālib Kalīm from Hama-

---

[131] MM 1787; Storey Nr. 1113; Marek/R 726.

[132] Ed. MAULVI MOHD. SHAFI 1926; MM 52; Storey Nr. 1115. A compatriot of his, Alā'ud-daula Kāmī Qazwīnī, had dedicated a *tadkira* called nafā'is al-ma'āṯir (= 973/1565, the date of its inception) to Akbar; MM 179; Storey Nr. 1101.

[133] Nabī's dustūr al-fuṣaḥā' about the technique of reciting the *qiṣṣa-yi Hamza* seems to be lost. A contemporary of his, Qiṣṣaḫʷān Ḥamdānī, wrote a Persian version of the story, called *zubdat ar-rumūz*, at the court of Muḥammad Quṭbshāh of Golconda, MM 1490. E 318 gives an account of the Persian, Turkish, Urdu, Hindi, Malay and Javanese versions of the Ḥamza-story. Miniatures in large size were painted under Akbar and are found in Vienna, Kunstgewerbemuseum as well as in various North American museums. An interesting ms. from Gujrat, late 15th century, with 189 miniatures in Berlin, Ms. or. fol. 4181, cf. R. ETTINGHAUSEN, Trudy IV 191/2; I. STCHOUKINE etc., Katalog Nr. 61; cf. also S. C. WELSH, l.c. p. 23ff.; and G. EGGER, Der Hamza-Roman, Wien 1969.

[134] MM 236; Storey Nr. 1169; ed. Calcutta 1918, 1927, 1939.

[135] MM 1625; BROWNE, l.c. IV 265ff. Ṣā'ib's *kulliyāt* were first printed Bombay 1882. Since they comprise ca. 300000 verses many selections have been made in Iran, India and Turkey. Cf. S. A. H. ABIDI, Ṣā'ib Tabrīzī Isfahānī, Life and Poetry, in: Yādnāme-yi Jan Rypka, Prague 1967.

dan (d. 1650), for a time poet laureate of the Mughal court.[136] He wrote *qaṣīdas* and *maṯnawīs* about every important event of the time, be it the fight of young 'Ālamgīr Aurangzeb with an infuriated elephant (a miniature of this event is also preserved),[137] the famine in the Deccan, or his visit to a papermill in Kashmir. Thus his poetry is a valuable document for our knowledge of Indian cultural life in the mid 17th century. He also composed a poetical chronicle, *šāhǧihānnāma*. Some lines in Kalīm's lyrical poetry are haunting in their pensive mood, and have been memorized time and again in India and Pakistan. Proverbial is the line in which he uses a motif dear to Indo-Persian poets, e.g. that of the 'Book of the days' which may have developed out of the idea of the 'Book of Destiny':

"We are unaware of the beginning and the end of the world:
The first and last page of this old book has fallen away!"

An he complains in traditional images—which are, however, artfully twisted —about the impossibility of true union:

"Not only flees in terror that young smiling rose from me:
The thorn in this desert drags away my skirt.
His hanging on to me is (like) the attachment of wave and shore:
Moment for moment with me, every wink fleeing from me . . ."

During his stay in Kashmir, the favourite summer resort of the Mughals, Kalīm became acquainted with Ġanī Kašmīrī (d. 1661), a typical representative of the Indian style at its most intricate.[138] Ġanī composed a beautiful elegy on Kalīm's death in which he compares his friend to Moses 'Kalīmullāh,' the pen being his miraculous rod, and gives the chronogram of his death in the line:

The Sinai of inner meaning became radiant by Kalīm = 1061/1650.

Mollā Tuġrā Mašhadī (d. before 1667) belongs to those authors who composed several books on Kashmir;[139] Ismā'īl Bīniš's romantic *maṯnawīs* likewise contain poetical descriptions of Kashmir and Lahore.[140] Of outstanding importance for the history of literature connected with this region is Muḥammad Aṣlaḥ's *taḏkira-yi šu'arā-yi Kašmīr* which, in its recent edition by H. Rashdi, is a veritable encyclopedia of poetry.[141] Among the poets in Kashmir we may also mention Naṣīb who composed in the mid 17th century his *rīšīnāma*, a bio-

---

[136] Dīvān ed. P. Bayḍā'ī, Teheran 1336 š.; E 309, 238; MM 834; Storey p. 572.

[137] In the Šahǧihānnāma in the Windsor Palace Collection.

[138] Dīvān, Lucknow 1931; MM 489; G. H. Tikku, Muḥammad Ṭāhir Ghanī: An Indian allegorist of the Persian Language, Studies in Islam II, Delhi 1966.

[139] E 336; MM 1797.

[140] E 298; MM 365.

[141] Muḥammad Aṣlaḥ, taḏkira-yi šu'arā'-yi Kašmīr, ed. H. Rashdi, Karachi 1967–68, with four vols. of addenda which constitute a fully documented anthology of poetry written about Kashmir and poets who were, in any form, connected with Kashmir.

graphical dictionary of Kashmiri saints.[142] Shortly before him, Muḥammad Ġauṯī of the Šaṭṭārī order (d. after 1633) had produced a *taḏkira* of 575—mainly Gujerati[143]—Muslim saints *(gulzār-i abrār)*; his spiritual ancestor Muḥammad Ġauṯ Gwaliōrī (d. 1562) should be mentioned in this connection as well, because his Persian work *ǧawāhir-i ḫamsa* 'Five jewels,' also extant in an Arabic translation, contains highly interesting material about mystical piety and Sufi practices of the 16th century, but has not yet been studied in full.[144]

Persian literature flourished not only in the centre of the Mughal Empire but also in the border provinces. Suffice it to mention the role of Sind—always a fertile soil for poetry—as a home of poets and historians in early Mughal times. The outstanding figure during this period is Mīr Maʿṣūm Nāmī (1537–1608) who first served the Tarkhans of Sind, but later associated himself with Khānkhānān 'Abdurraḥīm and Akbar.[145] Maʿṣūmī was sent as Akbar's ambassador to Iran; he excelled as a calligrapher who decorated memorial stones and buildings, i. a. in Fathpur Sikri, with exquisite inscriptions; he was likewise a physician who wrote medical treatises (and thus resembled his contemporary Firišta). His historical work *ta'rīḫ-i Maʿṣūmī* is one of the best accounts of the history of Sind from its conquest to the late 16th century. As a lyrical poet he was quite prolific. His most interesting poetical work is a *Ḫamsa* in which the epic *nāz ū niyāz*, or *ḥusn ū nāz*, is of particular importance since the famous Sindhi-Panjabi love romance of *Sassui Punhun* is recounted here for the first time in the form of a Persian *maṯnawī*.[146] A similar attempt was made by Maʿṣūmī's compatriote Idrākī Bēglārī (the author of a historical *bēglārnāma*) who, around 1620, versified the Sindhi folk tale of *Līlā Čanēsar* in Persian in the style of Ǧāmī's *Yūsuf ū Zulaiḫā*.[147] Later, the Panjabi tale of *Hīr Ranǧhā* was more than hundred times retold in different languages and elaborated in dozens of Persian *maṯnawīs*.[148]

At about the same time (1621) Muḥammad Ṭāhir Nisyānī wrote his *ta'rīḫ-i ṭāhirī*, a history of Sind which is interspersed with poetry,[149] complemented by Yūsuf Mīrak Sindī's *maẓhar-i šāhǧihānī* (1634)[150] and Sayyid Mīr Muḥammad Tattawī's *tarḫānnāma* (ca. 1655).[151]

---

[142] MM 1377; Storey Nr. 1312.

[143] MM 1170; Storey Nr. 1310.

[144] MM 1169; ZA p. 94f.; GAL II 418, S II 616.

[145] His ta'rīḫ-i Maʿṣūmī ed. U. M. Daudpota, Poona 1938; Sindhi transl. Hyderabad/Sind 1953; Urdu transl. Karachi 1959. A History of Sind from the 8th to the 16th century, transl. by R. H. Thomas, Bombay 1855; MM 1365; Storey p. 651f.

[146] About the Persian version of Sassui Punhun by Maulānā Ḥāǧǧī Muḥammad Riḍā'ī 1643 cf. E 253; MM 1239. In the 18th century, two Hindu authors worked on Persian versions of this tale.

[147] Maṯnawī Čanēsarnāma, ed. H. Rashdi, Karachi 1956; MM 690.

[148] E 253; cf. H. Hoshyarpuri, maṯnawiyāt-i Hīr Ranǧhā, Karachi 1957.

[149] Ed. N. B. Baloch, Hyderabad/Sind 1964; MM 1769; Storey p. 655.

[150] Ed. H. Rashdi, Hyderabad/Sind 1962; MM 1909.

[151] Ed. H. Rashdi, Hyderabad/Sind 1965; MM 785.

Historical writing continued to flourish at the Mughal court even more than before. The early Mughals could pride themselves with a historian like Ḫʷāndamīr (d. 1542),[152] the grandson of the noted Persian historian Mīrḫond (d. 1498), and the time of Akbar produced the two important contradictory historical accounts by Badā'ūnī and Abū'l-Faḍl as well as a number of other works. The interest in the prehistory of the Mughal rulers led Shāh Jihān to order a Persian translation of Timur's alleged autobiography, the *malfūẓāt-i Tīmūrī* (1637),[153] a book of doubtful authenticity; the comparison of the translation by Abū Ṭālib 'Ariḍī with the reliable *Ẓafarnāma* showed so many mistakes that a new version had to be written. The main court historians in Delhi during this period were Muʿtamad Khān (d. 1640), the author of an *iqbālnāma-yi ǧihāngīrī*,[154] and Mīrzā Muḥammad Ǧalāluddīn Ṭabāṭabā'ī who came to India in 1634; the latter composed among other works the *šiš fatḥ-i Kangrā*, six stylistically different accounts of the conquest of the fortress of Kangra—rhetorical concerns tended to overshadow content.[155] Muḥammad Ṣāliḥ Kanbōh's *'amal-i ṣāliḥ* 'Ṣāliḥ's work' or 'Pious Work' is considered among the good chronicles of the mid 17th century.[156] A historical work of strong Afghan bias was written under the auspices of Jihāngīr's favourite Khān Ǧihān Lōdī, e.g. Niʿmatullāh's *ta'rīḫ-i ḫānǧihānī wa maḫzan-i afǧānī*.[157]

The most famous historian of this period was to be Muḥammad Qāsim Hindūšāh called Firišta who belonged primarily to the Bijapur court. He served as an ambassador to Akbar in 1604 and died after 1624 in his mid fifties.[158] His *gulšan-i Ibrāhīm*, dedicated to his patron in Bijapur, however, is not a very trustworthy compilation of earlier material; its historical value is not as great as was formerly thought; yet the information gathered by Firišta about contemporary events has been often utilized by Western historians. It was the first comprehensive indigenous source of Indo-Muslim history to be edited and translated in Europe. Another historian of Gujrat was Sikandar ibn Muḥammad Mānǧhū whose *mir'āt-i Sikandarī* was completed in 1611.[159] In Golconda, too, Persian historiography flourished under the Quṭbshāhīs,

---

[152] Ed. Teheran 1333 s.; E 356; MM 923; Tauer/R 441 a.o.; Storey p. 104ff.

[153] MM 122; Storey p. 280ff.; transl. Major Ch. Stewart, London 1830.

[154] Ed. Calcutta 1865, Lucknow 1870, 1890, Allahabad 1931; MM 1344; Storey p. 561.

[155] MM 782; E 350 deals mainly with his dastūrnāma-yi kisrawī, a kind of Fürstenspiegel, and discusses similar works of Indian origin; Storey p. 566.

[156] Ed. Calcutta 1912–46; MM 1254; Storey p. 598.

[157] Ed. Dacca 1960–62; B. Dorn, History of the Afghans, London 1829–36; MM 1403; Storey Nr. 544. We may further mention 'Abdulḥamīd Lahaurī's pādšāhnāma, ed. Calcutta 1866–72; MM 20; Storey p. 575f.

[158] Bombay 1831, Lucknow 1864–5, 1905; first partly transl. by A. Dow, London 1768; History of the Rise of the Muhammadan Power in India, transl. J. Briggs, 4 vols. London 1829; MM 471; Storey Nr. 617; Tauer/R 448.

[159] Ed. Bombay 1831, 1890; English transl. F. L. Faridi, Bombay 1899; MM 1725; Storey p. 728.

whether we think of 'Alī ibn Ṭaifūr's *tuḥfa-yi Quṭbšāhī*, a 'mirror for princes' in eight chapters,[160] or of the interesting account of Ḫʷuršāh ibn Qubād known as *ta'rīḫ-i Ilčī Niẓāmšāh Quṭbī* which deals with the relations of the Shia kingdom of Golconda with the Safawids.[161] The *nisbatnāma-yi šahriyār*, an epical *maṯnawī* in 18000 couplets (ca. 1607)[162] and the epistolographic work by Ḥāǧǧī 'Abdul'alī Tabrīzī somewhat later are some specimens of Deccani Persian literature.[163] "Rather strangely, Bengal does not claim many historians of its own;"[164] otherwise there is no lack of provincial histories throughout the whole 17th and even 18th centuries.

Every art and science was well represented during the first half of the 17th century in Muslim India. 'Abdulḥakīm Siālkōtī (d. 1656)[165] wrote not only an Arabic commentary on the Quran but also on several dogmatic books, the principle one being on 'Aḍududdīn al-Īǧī's (d. 1355) *mawāqif*, the standard-work on dogmatics since the late 14th century. Other standard works on which Siālkōtī commented include Taftazānī's (d. 1389) works on logic, rhetoric, and metaphysics. To the commentaries of this scholar (like that on the *'aqā'id* of an-Nasafi, d. 1310), he added supercommentaries, condensations, explanations, almost suffocating the original with a thick layer of interpretations. Siālkōtī's most famous commentary is that on Ǧāmī's commentary to Ibn Ḥāǧib's *kāfiya*, the grammatical poem mentioned above. The indefatigable scholar was, moreover, the first to introduce some of Mollā Ṣadrā Shirazi's philosophical-mystical ideas into Indian environment.

A colleague of Siālkōtī was Mollā Maḥmūd of Jawnpur (d. 1651)[166] who wrote mainly philosophical textbooks, condensed them and commented again upon them, discussing problems like the relation of form and matter, etc.—Medicine flourished during those years, and Ibn Sīnā's medical work was commented upon and enlarged by Ḥakīm 'Alī Gīlānī (d. 1609).[167] The most comprehensive Persian work on medicine in India was written on Dārā Shikōh's instigation; other books on relevant subjects were composed in his brother Aurangzeb's time by Mīr Muḥammad Akbar Arzānī.[168]

One must also think of the dictionaries produced in the 17th century: 'Abdurrašīd Tattawī (d. 1658) with a critical approach wrote the Persian

---

[160] E 350; MM 201.

[161] Ed. Dr. M. H. Zaidi, New Delhi 1965; MM 924; Storey p. 113.

[162] MM 453.

[163] E 342; MM 8.

[164] Sharma, Bibliography p. 69.

[165] GAL II 417, S II 613, where also some of his disciples are enumerated; MM 18; ZA I 18, III 31, V 16, VI 14, IX 24.

[166] GAL II 420, S II 621; ZA IV 32, VI 13, IX 23; about philosophical works in Mughal India cf. GAL II 420, S II 620ff.

[167] GAL S II 626; ZA VII 3; about Arabic works on medicine in India cf. GAL II 421, S II 625; about Persian medical works in India cf. Tauer/R 475.

[168] Šāh Arzānī Muḥammad Akbar ZA VII 4; MM 1097: ṭibb-i akbarī; Nūraddīn-i Šīrāzī: ṭibb-i Dārā Šikōhī, MM 1424.

farhang-i Rašīdī, and the widely used Arabic-Persian *muntaḫab al-luġāt*. The *burhān-i qāṭi'* 'The Decisive Argument' was dedicated, in 1653, to the Quṭbshahī ruler by its author Muḥammad Ḥusain ibn Ḫalaf Tabrīzī.[170] These dictionaries continue the classical tradition—one has only to cite Saġānī's *al-'ubāb*, and the *qāmūs* of Firōzābādī who lived for a long time at Firozshah Tughluq's court.[171] The most important Arabic dictionary of the 18th century, the *tāǧ al-'arūs*, is likewise the work of an Indian scholar, viz. Sayyid Murtaḍā az-Zabīdī from Bilgram, the home-town of so many outstanding Islamic scholars.[172] Sayyid Murtaḍā was closely connected with Shāh Walīullāh Dihlawī before he left the country; he died in Cairo (1797) after finishing his indispensable dictionary and his voluminous commentary on Ġazzālī's *iḥyā' 'ulūm ad-dīn*, the *itḥāf as-sāda* 'Dedication of the sayyids.'

After the highly unorthodox reign of Akbar an 'Islamic' reaction set in. The leading Sunni—Ḥanafī—orthodoxy had always shown a marked aversion to the Shia whose influence waxed stronger with the immigration of poets and artists from Iran. Jihāngīr—though generally rather inclined to the Shiites for family reasons—yet had the leading Shia scholar of his time flogged to death in 1610 for alleged heresy; it was Nūrullāh Šūštarī, a prolific writer in Arabic on theology, religious biography, and many other subjects.[173]—The struggle against heterodoxy was mainly led by some members of the Naqšbandī order which, having greatly influenced the political and cultural life of Afghanistan and Central Asia since the mid 15th century, reached the Subcontinent shortly before 1600. The most weighty figure of this order is Aḥmad Sirhindī (1564–1624) who, although he composed quite a number of books in Arabic and Persian, exerted spiritual and political influence mainly through his letters.[174] 'Abdulḥakīm Siālkōtī hailed him as the *muǧaddid-i alf-i ṯānī* 'the reformer of the second millennium (after the Prophet)', a title accorded to him even in Turkish Naqšbandī circles. His emphasis upon the 'classical' interpretation of Sufism as opposed to the 'pantheistic' theories of *waḥdat al-wuǧūd* 'Unity of Being' was widely approved by later mystics in the Subcontinent. His theory that not 'Everything is He' but 'Everything is *from* Him' is in fact a more orthodox

---

169 Ed. Calcutta 1875; ed. M. ABBASI, Teheran 1337 š. = 1958; MM 69; Tauer/R 431; muntaḫab al-luġāt ed. J.H. TAYLOR, Calcutta 1816, and often; GAL II 416, S II 598; ZA 201ff.

170 Ed. M. MO'IN, Teheran 1330–42 š. = 1951–1963; M. ABBASI, Teheran 1336 š.; MM 374; Tauer/R 431.

171 Printed in four vols. Bulaq 1319 h/1901; GAL II 183, S II 234.

172 GAL II 288, S II 398; ZA I 47, II 28, III 63, IV 54, V 45, IX 44.

173 GAL S II 607; ZA I 12, II 11, III 29, V 11, VI 7, VII 3, IX 20; MM 1431; Storey Nr. 1574.

174 MM 155; Storey p. 988f.; ZA IV 25, V 13; Y. FRIEDMAN, Shaykh Ahmad Sirhindi, Montreal 1971. His letters were published Lucknow 1913 and often (maktūbāt-i imām-i rabbānī) in Persian as well as in Urdu and Turkish translations; the 206 Persian letters of his son and successor, Muḥammad Ma'ṣūm, maktūbāt-i Ma'ṣūm, Amritsar 1922, cf. MM 1203.

interpretation of God's transcendental Unity. The role Aḥmad assumed for himself and three of his descendants as the *qayyūm* 'through whom the whole world is kept in motion' could however lead to dangerous consequences. The Persian *rauḍat al-qayyūmīya* by Abū'l-Faiḍ Kamāluddīn Iḥsān, finished in 1751, as well as other hagiographical works by his followers explain these somewhat queer theories.[175]

The political role of Aḥmad and some of his successors in the decaying Mughal Empire should not be underrated. His teachings served as starting points for several reformist and fundamentalist movements in Northern India, culminating in the work of Shāh Waliullāh and his successors in the 18th century.

A contemporary of Aḥmad Sirhindi, with whom, however, he was not on very good terms, was 'Abdulḥaqq Dihlawī, known as *muḥaddiṯ* 'traditionalist' (1551–1642).[176] He popularized the study of the Prophetic tradition in India and laid the foundations of those schools of *ḥadīṯ* which were to remain centres of orthodox piety up to our day. Not less than sixteen of his Arabic and Persian books deal with *ḥadīṯ*, ten with history, including biographies of saints, and twelve with Sufism. He was a devout member of the Qādirī order which had gained a firm footing in India since the mid 15th century. That the *muḥaddiṯ* was also a poet in his own right (writing under the pen-name Ḥaqqī) goes almost without saying.

The Qādirī order gained its most prominent follower from the Mughal dynasty, despite the prior Čištī allegiance of the Mughals: Prince Dārā Shikōh (1615–1659), the first son of Shāh Jihān and Mumtāz Maḥal. He as well as his elder sister Jihānārā (1614–1689), a good writer in Persian, were initiated into the Qādirīya by Miān Mīr, a Sindhi, to whom Dārā dedicated a fine Persian biography *(sakīnat al-auliyā')*.[177] The prince devoted his time more to writing mystical books and letters (he was an excellent calligrapher as well) than to the duties of a future ruler, never serving as governor in the provinces.[178] His main

---

[175] rauḍat al-qayyūmīya, Ms. As. Soc. of Bengal, Calcutta, Urdu translation Lahore s.d.; cf. S. M. Ikram, rūd-i kauṯar, Lahore [4]1969; MM 98; Storey Nr. 1357.

[176] GAL II 416, S II 603; MM 21; ZA I 16, II 14, IV 29, V 15, VI 9, VIII 8; Storey Nr. 1298, p. 194, 181, 214, 427, 441; K. A. Nizami, ḥayāt-i šaiḫ 'Abdul Ḥaqq muḥaddiṯ-i Dihli, Delhi 1953; his aḫbār al-aḫyār Delhi 1309 h/1891, 1929, Deoband ca. 1968; his letters Delhi 1879. The historical work ta'rīḫ-i Ḥaqqī was enlarged by his son Nūr ul-Ḥaqq Mašriqī under the title zubdat at-ta'rīḫ, cf. ZA I 21, II 14, IX 25; MM 1429; Storey Nr. 616.

[177] sakīnat al-auliyā', ed. M. Jalālī Nā'īnī and Tara Chand, Teheran 1965.

[178] GAL II 420, S II 619; MM 402; Storey Nr. 1321; Marek/R 728; H. Blochmann, Facsimiles of several autographs of Jahangir, Shahjahan, and Prince Dara Shikoh ... JASBengal 1870; K. R. Qanungo, Dara Shukoh, Calcutta 1935; B. J. Hasrat, Dara Shikuh, Life and Works, Calcutta 1953; safīnat al-auliyā' ed. i.a. Lucknow 1872; Cawnpore 1900; for a full description cf. the Catalogue of the India Office Library, p. 273ff.; ḥasanāt al-'ārifīn, Delhi 1309 h/1892, engl. transl. Pandit Sheo Narain, J. of the Panjab Hist. Soc II, 1913–14; risāla-yi ḥaqqnumā, ed. Lucknow 1884, 1910, The Compass of Truth ... rendered into English by S. C. Basu, Allahabad 1912; risāla-yi ḥaqqnumā, maǧma' al-baḥrain, upnēkhat mandakm,

goal was, like that of Akbar, the reconciliation of Muslims and Hindus on the basis of mysticism. The *maǧma' al-baḥrain*, a small Persian prose work, shows by its very title that Dārā aimed at 'The Merging of the two Oceans,' e.g. Islam and Hinduism. But his importal achievement is the translation of 50 Upanishads into fluent Persian as the *sirr-i Akbar* 'The Greatest Secret'[179]—a most remarkable work which became one of the 'sacred scriptures' of European idealist philosophers after Anquetil Duperron translated it into Latin in 1801.

As a mystical poet, Dārā is not outstanding; his verses are comparatively simple, albeit rather intellectual. Important is his collection of biographies of saints, the *safīnat al-auliyā'*, and some of his theoretical works on Sufi definitions. He was, at the same time, a maecenas of Persian writing poets, and strange characters who did not at all fit orthodox ideals assembled around him. One among them, Sarmad, is especially worth mentioning: a Persian, or Armenian, Jew, he had studied Christian and Islamic theology, in part under the guidance of Mollā Ṣadrā of Shiraz. He was converted to Islam, became a merchant, lived for a while in Thatta, and then, probably as a result of an overwhelming love experience, gave up everything to become a dervish and joined Dārā's court.[180] He wandered about stark naked, defending himself with the lines:

"The One who gave you royal glory—
Gave us all the implements of confusion;
He gave a dress to everyone whose fault he saw—
To the immaculate ones He gave the dress of nudity."

And, following the tradition of some Sufi poets he takes Satan as the true confessor of Divine Unity, because he refused to prostrate himself before the created Adam:

"Sarmad, do not talk about Ka'ba and monastery,
Do not walk in the street of doubt like those gone astray!

---

ed. M. Jalāli Nā'inī, Teheran 1335 š.; maǧma' al-baḥrain or the Mingling of the two Oceans, ed. . . . with English translation. . . . by M. Mahfuz ul-Haq, Calcutta 1929; ṭarīqat al-ḥaqā'iq, ed. Gujranwala 1857 in the (incomplete) kulliyāt; Urdu transl. by A. A. Batalawi, Lahore 1923; Les entretiens de Lahore, ed. L. Massignon et Cl. Huart, JA CCIX, Paris 1926; L. Massignon et A. M. Kassim, Un essai de bloc islamo-hindou au XVII siècle: l'humanisme mystique du Prince Dārā, RMM LXIII, 1926.—A versified story depicting the relation between Dārā and Bābā Lāl is contained in Ḫʷaš's maṯnawī-yi kač-kulāh, 1794 (MM 250). About Dārā's dīvān cf. Maulvi Zafar Hasan, JRASBengal, Letters, vol. V, 1939.

[179] Ed. by Tara Chand and M. R. Jalālī Nā'inī, Teheran 1961; cf. E. Göbel-Gross, Sirr-i akbar, Die Upanishad-Übersetzung Dārā Shikohs, Phil. Diss. Marburg 1962.

[180] MM 1649; Marek/R 728f.; B. A. Hashmi, IC 1933, 1934 introduction and translation; rubā'iyāt, ed. and transl. by Fadl Mahmud Asiri, Shantiniketam 1950; cf. W. J. Fischel, Jews and Judaism at the Court of the Moghul Emperors in Medieval India, IC 1951; J. P. Asmussen, Studier i Jødsk-Persisk litteratur, Copenhaguen 1970.

Go, learn the art of (true) servantship from Satan:
Choose one direction of prayer, and do not prostrate yourself before anyone else."

Sarmad's Persian quatrains belong to the finest poems of this genre ever written. They reflect the feeling of a daring lover in the tradition of the martyr mystic al-Ḥallāǧ (ex. 922 in Bagdad), famous as an example of those who willingly accept suffering and death for the sake of their spiritual love. Sarmad himself was in fact put to death shortly after Dārā Shikōh had been executed by his brother 'Ālamgīr Aurangzeb in 1659.

Another member of Dārā's entourage was the Hindu Čandar Bhān Brahman (1582–1661), a disciple of 'Abdulḥakīm Siālkōtī, who became the private secretary to the heir apparent. He was a good poet in the mystically tinged style; his *munša'āt-i Brahman*, a group of official letter models, are eloquent and simple. His prose work *čār čaman-i Brahman* 'Brahman's Four Meadows' gives, in four parts, a lively inofficial account of the life in Lahore and Dehli during the rule of Shāh Jihān whom he had known well.[181]

Among the poets and writers connected with Kashmir in Dārā's days Muḥsin Fānī has often been mentioned.[182] He wrote Arabic religious works; the religious history *dabistān-i maḏāhib*, which is—probably wrongly—attributed to him, gives interesting impressions of the religions situation. As a lyrical poet in Persian, Fānī is rather mediocre. The prince's spiritual director, Mollā Shāh Badaḫšī (d. 1661) is famous as author of Arabic and Persian poetry mainly in honour of the Prophet, and of treatises on mystical problems, but has also poetically described the beauty of Kashmir.[183] It was to him that Princess Jihānārā devoted her hagiographical work.[184] Dārā's niece, Zeb un-Nisā' (d. 1689), deeply influenced by her uncle (to the dismay of her father) set out to write Arabic poetry at a tender age, but then concentrated upon Persian. Her lyrical *dīvān (dīvān-i Maḫfī)*—if it is genuine in its present form—contains 421 ġazals, some of them of rare beauty.[185] The free adaptation of her verses by J. D. Westbrook captures the mood of her lyrical effusions quite well:

"I have no peace, the quarry I, a Hunter chases me,
It is Thy memory;

---

[181] E 341–2 about his epistolography; MM 378; Marek/R 727f.; Iqbal Husain, Chandra Bhān Brahman, IC 1945.

[182] GAL S II 614; E 298; MM 447; Dīvān, ed. G. L. Tikku, Teheran 1342 s.; dabistān-i maḏāhib Calcutta 1224 h/1809, Lucknow 1881, Cawnpore 1904, engl. transl. by D. Shea and A. Troyer, London 1843 and later, thus New York, 1901. The book is probably the work of Mūbad Shah, cf. MM 1084.

[183] E 300; for his kulliyāt cf. Catalogue Bankipore III 112, 326.

[184] MM 770; Storey Nr. 1322; Urdu transl. Lucknow 1898.

[185] Dīvān-i Maḫfī, Cawnpore 1345 h/1926; maǧmū'a-yi ši'rhā, ed. by Javharizoda 1940, and with introduction by A. Sidqi, Stalinabad 1958; Shiblī Nu'mānī, sawāniḥ-i Zēb un-Nisā Begum, Lucknow s.d.; Fifty poems translated by Magan Lal and J. D. Westbrook, London 1913, Lahore ²1954; MM 1010; J. Bečka, Tajik Literature, in R 513; for the discussion about the authenticity of the dīvān cf. Catalogue Bankipore III 442.

I turn to flee, but fall; for over me he casts his snare,
  Thy perfumed hair.
Who can escape Thy prison? no mortal heart is free
  From dreams of Thee."

With the age of Aurangzeb the heyday of court poetry came to an end.[186] He abolished the title *malik as-šu'arā*. Poetry became, to use S. M. Ikram's expression, 'escapist,' seeking the lofty height of a world of imagination. A typical example is Ġanīmat Kanğōhī's (d. 1695) *maṯnawī nairang-i 'išq* 'Love's Magic' which ran completely counter to Aurangzeb's religious ideals.[187] One of the emperor's leading officials, Ni'mat Khān 'Ālī (d. 1709), who took part in the wars against Golconda and Bijapur, has described these events poetically and satirically. His *wāqi'āt-i Ni'mat Ḫān* and his memories won him the favour of the public who enjoyed his sometimes critical attitude towards the government, but resulted in Aurangzeb's antipathy towards the author.[188]

It is interesting to observe that the influence of the Naqšbandi order permeated even the literary scene during that period. Just as the great poets of the Timurid court at Herat in the 15th century, Ğāmī, Nawā'ī, and Ḥusain Wā'iẓ, were Naqšbandīs, one finds during the later Aurangzeb period and in the early 18th century a considerable number of poets affiliated with the Naqšbandīya even though this order is basically averse to the fine arts. One of these poets was Nāṣir 'Alī Sirhindī (d. 1697).[189] He filled his verses with such an amount of intellectual imagery and outlandish *concetti* that the great Persian poet Ḥazīn who reached India in the early 18th century exclaimed:

Of the poetry of Nāṣir 'Alī and the prose of Bēdil nothing can be understood; if I should bring them to Iran there would be nothing better to make my friends mock!

Nevertheless, some of Nāṣir 'Alī's verses are exquisite—if the reader only perseveres in struggling his way through the almost endless lines of intricate *ġazals* and *qaṣīdas*.

Nāṣir 'Alī is often mentioned together with Mīrzā Bēdil (d. 1721) who is generally recognized as the unsurpassable master of the Indian style and the most difficult writer of Muslim India in general.[190] Originating form the Turkish Arlas tribe, he was born in 'Aẓīmābād (Patna) in 1644; although he had no

---

[186] For the later development cf. SHAIKH IKRAM UL-HAQQ, ši'r-al-'ağam fī'l-Hind az awāḫir-i 'ahd-i Šāhğihānī tā asās-i Pākistān, Multan 1961.

[187] MM 490; BAUSANI, l.c. p. 62f.; Dīvān ed. GHULAM RABBANI AZIZ, Lahore 1958; nairang-i 'išq, ed. GH. R. AZIZ, Lahore 1962.

[188] E 337; MM 211; Storey 589ff., a.o.

[189] MM 222 and 1384; Dīvān lith. Lucknow 1844, 1281 h/1865.

[190] Ed. MAULĀNĀ ḪASTA, 4 vols, Kabul 1962–65; A. BAUSANI, Note su Mirza Bedil, Ann. Ist. Univ. Or. Napoli, NS VI 1957; Khwaja ABDULLAH AKHTAR, Bēdil kī šā'irī, Lahore 1952; ABDUL GHANI, Life and Works of Abdul Qadir Bedil, Lahore 1960; YASIN KHAN NIYAZI, in Oriental College Magazine 1932; MM 359; A. BAUSANI, Bēdil as a narrator, in: Yādnāme-yi Jan Rypka, Prague 1967; the most comprehensive survey of Bēdil studies: Bečka/R 515ff.

proper education, he was able to acquire wide learning and mystical knowledge. For a while he attached himself to several princes and travelled with them in the Eastern part of the Subcontinent. He then retired to Delhi where his modest tomb is still visited. His complete work, which has never been studied in full by a Western scholar, consists of 90.000 to 100.000 verses, many of them *maṯnawīs*. Bēdil was mainly interested in philosophical and mystical thought. His first *maṯnawī*, the *muḥīṭ-i aʿẓam* 'The Greatest Ocean,' is devoted to the development of creation: the world which is not distinct from the pre-eternal Divine essence, comes, like wine, into fermentation and this results in a development process that culminates in man, for in man the different manifestations of being become aware of themselves and man can consciously move forward and upward, eventually to reach the Divine light. This idea of a constant upward movement in which everything participates (not only the wayfarer travels but the way as well) was known from classical Sufi poetry (Sanā'ī, 'Aṭṭār, Rūmī). In its new formulation, it made Bēdil one of the favourite poets of Iqbāl who found his own ideas of the innate dynamics of life preformed in the former's verses.

Bēdil's *Čāhar ʿunṣur* 'The Four Elements,' completed in 1704, consists of four books. It is a mixture of poetry and prose in which the author gives much autobiographical data, including notes about his spiritual experiences. His *dīvān* and his *rubāʿīyāt* are voluminous, as are his letters many of which are addressed to Šukrullāh Khān. There is not a single poetic technique and rhetorical word-play which he does not fully master; J. Rypka has suggested that the breathtaking difficulty of his style can perhaps be explained from his wish to hide unorthodox ideas in an uncongenial, nay inimical environment. Expressions like *šikast* 'broken' or *ḫamyāza*, lit. 'yawning' but then 'insatiable thirst' (the thirst of the shore to embrace the ocean, as Kalīm has put it) permeate Bēdil's poetry—a poetry which has never been popular in Iran, but was and still is so lovingly read in Afghanistan and Muslim Central Asia that he is considered the major Tāǧik poet of classical times. Bēdil's verses are still being taught in schools in remote Afghan places, and are known to every educated person.[191] In India he was similarly well-liked. Ġālib and Iqbāl gladly acknowledged their indebtedness to him. In Europe, however, he has remained comparatively unknown owing to the almost unsurpassable difficulties of his style. Yet he does amply reward the diligent reader with verses of weird beauty that are sometimes reminiscent of post-expressionist poetry.

A few of his simpler lines may illustrate the strange blending of restlessness and hopelessness which permeates his verses which use the traditional images in a highly 'broken' and intellectualized way:

"Even the dead man thinks of resurrection—
How difficult is it to rest!"

---

[191] Cf. P. Centlivres, Un bazar de l'Asie Centrale: Tashqurgan; Wiesbaden 1971, p. 60.

But he wants no rest:

"It is said that Paradise is eternal rest—
A place where the heart no longer trembles with a scar—what kind of place is that!"
"Out of longing and want for you the shifting sand dunes in the breast of the desert are trembling like a helpless heart."

This is a beautiful *ḥusn-i ta'līl*, a 'phantastic aetiology,' in which the movement of the *rēg-i rawān*, the wandering dunes, is explained as the heart-beat of the longing desert.

"We have administered the ritual washing of the martyrs with the water of the sword—
Our head learns prostating only in front of the *miḥrāb* of the sword."

This beginning of a *ġazal* with the rhyme-word 'sword' seems typical of the tendency towards more and more cruel images; it forecasts some of Ġālib's most sinister verses.—According to Muslim faith, the martyrs who have been slain in the way of God are not to be washed like normal dead bodies; they are, so to speak, purified by shedding their blood. The whole verse plays on concepts from the ritual sphere (martyr, washing, prostration, *miḥrāb*).

Another idea often expressed by Bēdil and his contemporaries is contained in the following lines:

"Here, the morning of old age results in giving up one's hope;
Here, the woof and warp of the shroud is the white hair."

The morning is generally the time of hope and joy, but the whiteness of the hair which announces the 'morning of old age' induces man into hopelessness; even more, the white hair that falls from the head, turns one by one into the yarn for the shroud.

The age of Aurangzeb produced, naturally, noted legal work; such as that of Mollā Ǧiwān (d. 1717) who wrote on Islamic law and exegesis.[192] An highly important achievement was the completion of the *fatāwā-yi 'Ālamgīrī* in which the leading authorities of Ḥanafi law participated so that this Arabic work became one of the most valuable sources for our knowledge of Islamic institutions in later Mughal times.[193] One of the leading judges of the kingdom under Aurangzeb was Muḥibbuddīn Bihārī (d. 1707), the author of numerous Arabic works, i.a. on philosophy; his *sullam al-'ulūm*' Staircase of Sciences' has served many generations of Indian students as an introduction into logic.[194]

Aurangzeb's own letters give a deep insight into the problems of this last great Mughal ruler and show that he, like his ancestors, was capable of writing a forceful and elegant style. Though he later banned the composition of official

[192] GAL S II 612; ZA I 37, III 41.

[193] About Ḥanafi *fiqh* in Mughal times cf. GAL II 417, S II 604f. The fatāwā-yi 'ālamgīrī ed. in 6 vols. Bulaq 1276 h/1859; about its authors MM 1183, 1189, 1410, 1418; about Quranic science in Mughal times cf. GAL S II 610ff.

[194] GAL II 421, S II 622; MM 1286; ZA III 38 his main work on fiqh, musallam at-ṯubūt, V 24, VI 25.

historical writing, several important historical works were written during his early day, thus Muḥammad Kāẓim ibn Amīn's *'ālamgīrnāma,*[195] Musta'idd Khān's *ma'āṯir-i 'ālamgīrī,*[196] and 'Āqil Khān Rāzī's *wāqi'āt-i 'ālamgīrī.*[197] Another chronicle, called *muntaḫab al-lubāb,* was compiled by Muḥammad Hāšim Ḫāfī Khān (ca. 1665–ca. 1733),[198] 'the prince of plagiarists.'[199] This historian spent the later part of his life in the Deccan where he became *dīvān* of Nizamulmulk in 1713. At Golconda, he enjoyed the company of the vizier 'Abdurrazzāq Šāhnawāzḫān Ṣamṣāmuddaula, the author of the useful politico-cultural history *ma'āṯir al-umarā'.*[200] The manuscript of this valuable book was nearly lost when Ṣamṣāmuddaula's house was looted by his political enemies in 1758, but it was saved thanks to the efforts of Āzād Bilgrāmī, one of the outstanding writers of the 18th century.

This Mīr Ġulām 'Alī Āzād was born in 1704 in a distinguished family of Bilgram. His maternal grandfather was 'Abdulǧalīl Bilgrāmī (d. 1725), for a time at Aurangzeb's court, then newswriter in Gujrat, later in Sind.[201] He was a versatile poet in Arabic who knew how to use intelligently every conceivable rhetorical possibility. He was especially famous for skilful chronograms on historical events—a poetic form that reflects the main trend in 18th century Muslim intellectual games. Besides Arabic and Persian, he mastered Hindi and Turkish.—As to his grandson Āzād[202] 'the tongue is incapable to describe the greatness and perfection of that person.' He came to Sehwan, met 'Ali Ḥazīn at Bhakkar, performed the pilgrimage in 1737 and studied the *ṣaḥīḥ* of Buḫārī under Muḥammad Ḥayāt Sindhi, one of the numerous Indian Muslim scholars who had retired to Mecca. In 1740, Āzād reached Aurangabad where he became a close friend of the ruling families, mainly of the vizier Ṣamṣāmuddaula. He died in 1786.

---

[195] Ed. Calcutta 1865–73; MM 1194; Storey p. 586f.

[196] Ed. Calcutta 1870–73; transl. H. VANSITTART, Calcutta 1785, J. SARKAR, Calcutta 1947; MM 1343; Storey p. 593.

[197] Ed. Lahore 1936, Aligarh 1946; MM 264; Storey p. 584; 'Āqil Khan was also a poet who wrote some *maṯnawīs* on Indian love stories.

[198] Ed. Calcutta 1860, 1909–25, many extracts in translation MM 883; Storey p. 468.

[199] Sharma, Bibliography p. 47.

[200] MM 1669; Storey Nr. 1471; the *ma'āṯir* were enlarged by his son 'Abdul Ḥayy Sārim (MM 24), and thus edited by MAULVI ABDUR RAHIM and MIRZA ASHRAF ALI, Calcutta 1888–91; transl. H. BEVERIDGE, Calcutta 1911, rev. and completed by B. PRASHAD, 3 vols., Calcutta 1941.

[201] MM 25; Storey p. 721f.; ZA VI 28; X 8, XI 9; MAQBUL SAMDANI, Ḥayāt-i Ǧalīl, Allahabad 1929. The versatile author even versified an Arabic-Persian, Turki-Hindi dictionary . . .!

[202] GAL S II 600; AZ II 26, VIII 14, X 12, XI 13; MM 287; Storey Nr. 1162, 1362; SAYYID WAJAHAT HUSAIN, JRASBengal 1936, 119f. Āzād's *dīvāns* were edited in several forms Hyderabad/Deccan, subḥat al-marǧān lith. Bombay 1903; ma'ātir al-kirām Hyderabad 1910; ḫizāna-yi 'āmira Cawnpore 1871, 1900, Lucknow s.d.; sarw-i Āzād Lahore 1913.

Āzād's literary production is extremely large. It ranges from an Arabic commentary on Buḫārī's *ṣaḥīḥ* to poetry in honour of the Prophet which gained him the honorific title Ḥassān al-Hind, recalling Muhammad's panegyrist Ḥassān ibn Ṯābit. He wrote the *ma'āṯir al-kirām*, biographies of 150 important inhabitants of his home-town, and the *sarw-i Āzād* 'The free Cypress' (or: 'Āzād's Cypress'), a biographical dictionary of 143 poets who were born in or visited India, including eight poets who wrote in *rēḫta*, i.e. Urdu. His strangest book is the Arabic *subḥat al-marǧān fī āṯār Hindūstān*, 'The coral-rosary about India,' an attempt to prove, by Prophetic traditions, that India is the real homeland of prophecy—its argumentation sounds not very convincing to a modern reader. The second chapter of the *subḥa* is devoted to biographies of outstanding Indian Muslims, the third one contains a discussion of literary beauties, partly in relation to Indian ideals of poetical beauty. The fourth part explains expressions of love in Indian and Arabic poetry. Āzād's style abounds in rarities; there is not a single figure of speech which he has not used. A model of his artificial embellishments is the *mir'āt al-ǧamāl* 'Mirror of Beauty' in which he describes—in a form adopted from Indian culture—the parts of the beloved's body in 150 verses with most unusual comparisons. Thus he says about the 'lock of hair' with four quite witty comparisons:

"Are these two locks of hair on the whiteness of her cheeks,
or two marginal columns on the book of beauty,
or two nights of the two *'īd* festivals that came together,
or are these two of the Seven Panegyrics, hung on the Ka'ba?"

The comparison of the face with a book is often used, the black tresses are compared to lines of writing; the face is as radiant as the two religious festivals in the Muslim year, preceded by the nights full of expectation; the *mu'allaqāt* are the seven most famous pre-Islamic Arabic poems which, according to legends, were suspended from the central sanctuary in Mecca—the face is compared to this sanctuary from which the poetry-like tresses are hanging so that men may marvel at their beauty.

A good example of Āzād's skill in using the 'phantastic aetiology' is his elegant Persian verse about the opening rose:

"The return of royal glory is finally towards indigence—
For the crown of the rose-bud became a beggar's bowl,"

That he equalled his grandfather in the art of chronograms goes almost without saying. Āzād's main historical work is the *ḫizāne-yi 'āmira*, 'The florishing Treasure,' an account of 135 interesting personalities who lived at the court of the Nizam till 1762. It is an important source of South Indian history since the author, who was always in contact with the leading officials, had been an eye witness of many of the events he describes.

One of Āzād Bilgrāmī's pupils was a Hindu, Lakšmī Narayān Šafīq (d.

1745);[203] he wrote poetry in Persian and Urdu and composed a historical and topographical description of India for his British patron *(ḥaqīqathā-yi Hind)*. He thus ushered in a period in which travel accounts and geographical books became increasingly popular with both Indian writers and British officials. Šafīq's *gul-i ra'nā* 'Lovely Rose' is a widely used *taḏkira* of Indian poets who wrote in Persian, while the *šām-i ġarībān* 'The Evening of the Strangers' contains information on Persian poets who visited India.

The number of biographical handbooks grew almost infinitely during the 18th century. Making up for the lack of proper inspiration, the writers preferred to collect and organize the available material and thus preserved many verses which would otherwise be lost. One of the most famous *taḏkiras* is that by 'Alī Ḥazīn who left Iran owing to the Afghan invasion but met in India the same, and even worse, tribulations, wars, and internal feuds all of which he has touchingly described in his autobiography *taḏkirat al-aḥwāl*.[204] (The genre of autobiographies became more prominent during the following decades). 'Alī Ḥazīn, who died in Benares in 1766, composed not only lyric and epic poetry, but also religious writings, such as a commentary on Suhrawardī Maqtūl's (ex. 1191) work. His *taḏkirat al-mu'āṣirīn* deals very critically with more than a hundred contemporary poets, as he disliked the Indian style intensely. But just as Ḥazīn criticized his Indian colleagues whose poetry he considered too cumbersome (in contrast to his own sweet flowing style) he himself was severely attacked by Sirāǧuddīn 'Alī Khān Ārzū (d. 1756) in his *tanbīh al-ġāfilīn* 'Admonition of the Heedless.'[205] This Khān Ārzū set about correcting and enlarging the Persian dictionary *burhān-i qāṭi'* in his *sirāǧ al-luġāt* 'Lamp of Dictionaries' and composed also a *čirāġ-i hidāyat* 'Candle of Guidance' about more recently used Persian expressions. He excelled in compiling commentaries and biographies, and his influence upon the development of Urdu poetry is well known.

Among the *taḏkiras* during the post-Aurangzeb period we many mention the following as most useful—though partly very voluminous: Šēr Khān Lōdī's *mir'āt al-ḫayāl* (1960),[206] Binraban Dās Ḫošgū's *safīna-yi Ḫošgū* (1734),[207] Wālih Dāġistānī's (d. 1756) *riyāḍ aš-šu'arā'*,[208] 'Ali Beg Āḏar's *ātaškada* 'Fire-

[203] MM 1662; Storey Nr. 1165, cf. p. 476f.; šām-i ġarībān, ed. maǧalla-yi Urdu 4/1969, the title refers to eve of tenth of Muharram.

[204] GAL S II 613; E 310; R 308; Tauer/R 451; MM 629; Storey Nr. 1150; Browne, l. c. IV 115–8, 277–81; Kulliyāt Lucknow 1923 h/1876; Cawnpore 1893; ta'rīḫ-i Ḥazīn, Isfahan 1332 š.; F. C. Belfour, The Life of Shaikh Mohammad Ali Hazin, London 1830, and ed. of his ta'rīḫ-i aḥwāl bi-taḏkira-yi ḥāl, London 1831; also later editions. Cf. Sarfaraz Khan Khattak, Shaikh Muhammad Ali Hazin, His Life, Time, and Works, Lahore 1944.

[205] MM 269; Storey Nr. 1149; Tauer/R 431; E 214f. gives a survey of *taḏkiras* in general.

[206] Calcutta 1831, Bareilly 1848, Bombay 1906; MM 1693; Storey Nr. 1135.

[207] MM 363; Storey Nr. 1139.

[208] MM 1864; Storey Nr. 1147.

temple'[209] and Nawwāb 'Ali Ibrāhīm Ḫalīl's *gulzār-i Ibrāhīm* and *ṣuḥuf-i Ibrāhīmī*.[210]—Bhagwān Dās Hindī (d. after 1805) left, besides two *maṯnawīs* and two *dīvāns*, a book on Persian poets in India, the *safīna-yi Hindī*.[211]

It is small wonder that during the hopeless situation of the floundering Mughal Empire after Aurangzeb's death (1707) in the turmoil of incessant internal and external attacks and continuous destruction, Persian literature somewhat stagnated. Truly great poetry needed a new medium, which proved to be Urdu; yet Sindhi, Panjabi, and Pashto also developed an impressive literature of their own. To be sure, the theologians and mystics in Delhi and elsewhere continued writing in the classical Islamic languages. Even the man who is usually counted among the 'four pillars of Urdu', Mīr Dard, composed the largest part of his mystical poetry and prose in a very poetic Persian interspersed with chapters in powerful Arabic.[212] Dard's father, Muḥammad Nāṣir 'Andalīb, was a mystic and writer in his own right.[213] He had been a disciple of the Naśqbandī master Shāh Sa'dullāh Gulšan, that prolific poet who was largely responsible for Walī Deccani's stay in Delhi and thus instrumental in the introduction of Urdu poetry in the North. Shāh Gulšan was in turn a friend of Bēdil and Nāṣir 'Ali Sirhindī. Thus the tradition of the *sabk-i hindī* goes without interruption through the Naqšbandī poets of Dehli. Almost the same can be said for Maẓhar Ǧānǧānān, again much more a Persian than an Urdu writer (his spiritual letters are particularly worth reading). He, again considered one of the 'four pillars of Urdu', was, like Dard, a stern Naqšbandi mystic and anti-Shia.[214]

The theologian who expressed the views of his contemporaries most clearly in his Arabic and Persian writings was Shāh Walīullāh of Delhi[215] whose father

[209] MM 290 and 976; Storey Nr. 1170; JRAS VII 345–92; lith. Calcutta 1249/1833; Bombay h/1860; ed. H. S. Nasiri, Teheran 1337–41 s.

[210] MM 206; Storey Nr. 1176, p. 700f.; the gulzār-i Ibrāhīm ed. by Dr. S. Qadri, Aligarh 1934. For further taḏkiras cf. Muḥammad Afḍal Sarḫoš, kalimāt aš-šu'arā, Madras 1951; MM 1648; Storey Nr. 1132; and Kišan Čand Iḫlāṣ, hamīša bahār, MM 693; Storey Nr. 1139.

[211] Ed. Shāh M. 'Aṭā', Patna 1958; MM 344; Storey Nr. 1183.

[212] 'ilm ul-kitāb Delhi 1308 h/1890; čahār risāla Bhopal 1310 h/1892; dīvān-i fārsī Delhi 1309 h/1891; MM 403. Cf. Dr. Haydar Akhtar, Hʷāǧa Mīr Dard, taṣawwuf aur šā'irī, Aligarh 1971; A. Schimmel, Mir Dard's Gedanken über das Verhältnis von Mystik und Wort, in: Festgabe deutscher Iranisten zur 2500-Jahrfeier, Stuttgart 1971; the same, A sincere Muhammadan's way to God, G. S. F. Brandon Memorial Volume, Manchester 1973.

[213] Nāla-yi 'Andalīb, 2 vol., Bhopal 1310 h. 1892.

[214] MM 800; his anthology ḫarīṭa-yi ǧawāhir and his *dīvān* together printed Cawnpore 1271h/1855, Lahore 1922; kalimāt-i ṭayyibāt Delhi 1891; ḫuṭāṭ (letters), ed. Khaliq Anjum, Delhi 1962; hagiographical works about him and his branch of the Naqšbandīya: Na'īm Allāh Bahrā'īčī, bišārat-i maẓharīya and ma'mūlāt-i maẓhariya, Cawnpore 1867, Lahore 1893; cf. MM 1357; Storey Nr. 1375.

[215] GAL II 418, S II 614; ZA I 44, II 23, III 54, IV 46, V 36, X 10, XI 12; MM 1857; Storey Nr. 1352, p. 21ff. a.o.; his autobiography JASBengal 1912, 161–75; A. Bausani, Note su Shah Waliullah di Dehli, Ann. Ist. Orient. Univ. Napoli, NS X, 1961; K. A. Nizami, Šāh Walīullāh kē siyāsī maktūbāt, Aligarh 1950; ḥuǧǧat

had cooperated in the compilation of the *fatāwā-yi 'ālamgīrī*. Walīullāh's most significant work is the translation of the Quran into Persian—a translation which is regarded as the best ever made in this language. It was inspired by the feeling of this great theologian (who had been trained in Mecca) that the Muslim community of India should be able to understand the Sacred Writ so that they would act according to its injunctions without the mediation of numerous commentaries and more or less uninspired explanations. Shāh Walīullāh also composed several books on the principles of exegesis; he wrote about the historical development of the legal schools in Islam and tried to bridge the gap between the various legal and mystical interpretations of that religion. Large is the number of his writings on Prophetic traditions, but his main work, in Arabic, is the *ḥuǧǧat Allāh al-bāliġa*, 'The Excellent Proof of God,' a summary of his religious thought. Shāh Walīullāh who actively, if unsuccessfully, participated in Indian politics by inviting the Afghan leader Aḥmad Shāh Durrānī to support the faithful against the attacks of the Sikh and Mahrattas, stressed in his religious writings mainly the practical aspects of Islam. Still, in some of his mystical speculations he reached an amazing height and like Aḥmad Sirhindi, he felt himself to be a God-chosen instrument for the amelioration of the conditions of the Muslims. Like most Naqšbandīs, he was very much biassed against the numerous and influential Shia population in India, and even translated one of Aḥmad Sirhindi's anti-Shia works into Arabic. That he, too, now and then indulged in poetry is natural.

Shāh Walīullāh's tradition was carried on first by his sons 'Abdul'azīz[216] and Rafī' uddīn,[217] both prolific writers in Arabic who turned to Urdu, however, for their translations of the Quran. Through them, his ideas were led to the fundamentalist freedom-fighters of the early 19th century who wrote several important but little known books in Arabic and Persian on religious topics and mystical theology (especially Shāh Isma'īl Šahīd, d. 1829).[218]

Since the Persian style became increasingly more involved and studded with rare expressions and newly coined words, the compilation of new lexicographic works was considered necessary in the 18th century. Of particular note among them are the *farhang-i ānandrāǧ* by Munšī Muḥammad Bādšāh which comprises Arabic, Persian, and Turkish, and the enormous *bahār-i 'aǧam* and the *ǧawāhir al-ḥurūf* by Tēk Čand Bahār, (d. 1775), a pupil of Khān Ārzū.[219]

Allāh al-bāliġa, Bareilly 1868; Cairo s.d. (ca. 1955). tuḥfat al-muwaḥḥidīn, Delhi 1894; al-balāġ al-mubīn, Lahore 1890; his views about iǧtihād transl. by Daud Rahbar, MW XLV 1955. The Waliullah Academy, Hyderabad/Sind under its director Gh. Mustafa Qāsimī has published a considerable number of books and treatises of Shāh Walīullāh during the last ten years.

216 GAL S II 615; ZA I 52, II 33, IV 57, V 53, VI 56, VIII 16, IX 18, X 15, XI 16; MM 10; Storey Nr. 40, Nr. 299, Nr. 1586a.o.

217 GAL S II 850; ZA I 54, VI 60, X 18, XI 17; MM 1499.

218 ZA II 34, V 56, X 17.

219 MM 306; Tauer/R 432.

Among the leading scholars in the traditional fields of Islamic learning we must underscore the importance of 'Abdul'alā' Thānawī (d. 1745) whose *kašf-i iṣṭilāḥāt-i funūn* is an indispensable work for everyone interested in Islamic scholarship.[220] Further there is the great scholar—for a time at the Lucknow court—'Abdul'alī surnamed Baḥr al-'ulūm (d. 1819)[221] to whom we owe, among numerous other works, one of the best commentaries ever written on Rūmī's *Maṯnawī*,—and already in previous centuries more than a dozen voluminous commentaries on this cornerstone of mystical poetry in Islam had been composed in the Subcontinent, just as the imitations, translations and excerpts from the *Maṯnawī* were almost innumerable.[222]

One of the strongholds of Islamic studies was Sind.[223] Among the Persian poets 'Abdulḥakīm 'Aṭā' Tattawī (1627–1724), a staunch Shia, excelled as a satirist. His verses give a vivid impression of the worsening conditions in the province and thus also serve as historical sources.[224] Another Shia writer of Thatta was Muḥsin (d. 1750) who composed, among other works, a *maṯnawī* on the Twelve Imāms and a *marṯīya* in *maṯnawī* form.[225]

Arabic literature flourished in Sind once more during the early 18th century when some theologians of Naqšbandi persuasion tried to restore Islam to its pristine purity and wrote for this propose simple Sindhi verses on religious topics on the one hand, and Arabic works about Islam on the other. The leader of the movement was Maḫdūm Muḥammad Hāšim (d. 1760), the author of more than 125 works.[226] His mystically inclined colleague Muḥammad Mu'īn Maḫdūm Thōrā (d. 1748) who wrote Persian poetry under the pen-name Taslīm and Urdu as Bēragī, composed many Arabic books on Prophetic traditions, of which the *dirāsāt al-labīb* 'Lessons of the Persevering' is best known.[227] Maḫdūm Muḥammad Hāšim accused him, probably correctly, of forgery of *ḥadīṯ*.

Sind has always been a country of saints; but its vast mystical literature is almost unkown outside the country since most of the treatises are still in manuscript.[228] The *tuḥfat aṭ-ṭāhirīn* 'Gift of the Pure' by Muḥammad A'ẓam Tattawī

---

220 GAL II 421, S II 628; ZA IX 41.

221 GAL II 421, S II 624; ZA II 32, III 70, IV 56, V 50, VI 55, VII 14.

222 About imitations of the Maṯnawī and commentaries cf. E 301, further R. A. NICHOLSON's introduction to his edition of the Maṯnawī, London 1925–1940; A. SCHIMMEL, Maulana Jalaluddin Rumi's Influence on Muslim Literature, in: Güldeste, Aspects of Mevlâna, Konya 1971.

223 H. S. SADARANGANI, Persian Poets of Sind, Karachi 1956.

224 Dīvān, ed. M. RASHID BURHANPURI, Karachi 1966; hašt bihišt, ed. H. RASHDI, Karachi 1963.

225 Dīvān, ed. HABIBULLAH RUSHDI, Hyderabad/Sind 1963.

226 GAL S II 612; ZA I 43, III 53, V 34; Storey II S. 207. A complete list of his works in takmila (cf. note 233), p. 43f., 707.

227 ed. M. A. RASHID NU'MANI, Karachi 1957; complete list of his works in takmila 185 f; 234.

228 A survey of Persian hagiographic works from Sind is given by H. RASHDI in his edition of Sayyid 'Abdul Qādir Tattawī, ḥaqīdat al-auliyā', Hyderabad/Sind 1967; cf. MM 54.

(late 18th century) is useful for both hagiography and the historical geography of the Thatta area.[229] One of the major Persian poets of Sind during the 18th century was the Suhrawardi saint of Rohri, Mīr Ǧān Muḥammad Riḍwī (d. 1754). He wrote glowing verses about the manifestation of the Divine in human form and also about the martyr mystic Shāh 'Ināyat of Jhok (executed in 1718 for alleged rebellion).[230]

The most important representative of Persian literature in Sind was Mīr 'Alī Šīr Qāni', a member of the Sayyid Šukrullāh family (1727–1789).[231] He acted, for a while, as court poet of the Kalhoro dynasty and wrote more than 30.000 verses, many of them rather insipid primarily because of his use of exaggerated rhetorical games. Qāni''s fame will rest upon the *maqālāt aš-šu'arā* (1759) which contains short biographical notes of all poets who were in any way connected with Sind. His *tuḥfat al-kirām* 'Gift of the Noble' dealing with the scholars and theologians of the country, is likewise filled with valuable information. Qāni' has also devoted a charming booklet to Makli Hill, the vast cimetery near Thatta, and its importance for poets and mystics. Members of his family, like his son Mā'il,[232] and later Ibrāhīm Tattawī,[233] continued the tradition of *taḏkira* writing which flourished all over India.

Bengal did not lack good writers in Persian either—Murshidabad was a centre of Islamic learning. That knowledge of Persian was still considered natural even among the Hindus, is proved by the Persian treatises of Ram Mohan Roy, the well-known reformer of the early 19th century. In later years the poet Nassāḫ from Calcutta is mentioned among the better writers of Persian, whereas the classical tradition was maintained, into the present century, by the Suhrawardi family whose most noted member 'Ubaidullāh Suhrawardī (d. 1885) wrote Persian poetry and encouraged Islamic studies. Numerous Indian scholars assisted the British in translating and editing classical Persian works of general interest during the whole 19th century, as can been seen in the works published in the Bibliotheca India in Calcutta.

The interest in Arabic literature, even outside theology, philosophy, and related fields, never died in the Subcontinent. In 1715 Abū Bakr ibn Muḥsin composed an Indian counterpart to the Arabic masterpiece of rhetorical ingenuity, the *maqāmāt al-Ḥarīrī*, called *al-maqāmāt al-hindīya*.[234] A typical example of the sympathy for Arabic belles-lettres is *al-manāqib al-ḥaidarīya*, which was

[229] Ed. B. A. Durrani, Karachi 1956; MM 1128; Storey Nr. 1370.

[230] Cf. A. Schimmel, Shah 'Ināyat of Jhok, in: Liber Amicorum, Studies in Honour of C. J. Bleeker, Leiden 1969.

[231] MM 223; Storey Nr. 165, 656, 1158, 1373; tuḥfat ul-kirām, ed. H. Rashdi, Hyderabad/Sind 1971, vol. I; Sindhi transl. id. 1957, Urdu transl. id. 1959; J. Postans, Translation of the Tohfat ul-Kiram, a history of Sind, JASBengal, XIV; maqālāt aš-šu'arā', ed. H. Rashdi, Karachi 1957 (with extensive bibliography); Maklīnāma, ed. H. Rashdi, Hyderabad/Sind 1967. — Cf. Sadarangani 124ff.

[232] kulliyāt, ed. M. A. Abbasi and Habibullah Rushdi, Karachi 1959.

[233] takmila maqālāt aš-šu'arā, ed. H. Rashdi, Karachi 1958.

[234] ZA X 7.

composed by Aḥmad ibn Muḥammad aš-Šīrwānī in honour of the king of Oudh. It was the first book to be printed in the letter-press which Sultan Ḥaidar Ġāzī set up in Lucknow[235] A rather uninspiring work, following the classical pattern of anthologies with anecdotes and poetic descriptions, it is worth mentioning for an amusing detail: it contains an Arabic *marṯiya* which—according to the fanciful author—the ruler's favourite elephant used to recite on the day of 10th Muḥarram, and the onomatopoetical lines which imitate the elephant's trumpeting in long stressed *wāāhh Ḥusaināāāāāh* . . . are, to say the least, quite unusual.

It is further worth mentioning that towards the end of the 19th century the husband of the Rānī of Bhopal, Ṣiddīq Ḥasan Khān, under whose auspices numerous Arabic and Persian books on Islamic topics were printed in Bhopal, composed among other theological books a voluminous Arabic work on the status of women in Islam.[236]

As to Persian, it remained the language of high literature even after the British abolished it as the official language in 1835. Although Urdu had largely replaced Persian as the language of poetry, two of the greatest poets of Indian Islam used this language to express their deepest ideas—both of them, interesting enough, admirers of Bēdil. They are Mīrzā Asadullāh Ġālib and Muḥammad Iqbāl.

Ġālib's Persian poetry, though much larger than his Urdu *dīvān*, is often not appreciated properly, even though he himself regarded it as his truly 'colourful' poetry as contrasted with his 'colourless' Urdu verses.[237] His mastery of the most difficult forms led him to disregard all of his Persian writing colleagues in the Subcontinent (famous is his literary feud with the admirers of the Bengali poet Qatīl[238] in Calcutta between 1827 and 1829); his pride induced him to compose a book against the reputed dictionary *burhān-i qāṭi'*. One of the Bengali scholars of Persian, Maulwī Aḥmad 'Alī from Dacca who edited Persian sources for the Asiatic Society of Bengal and composed a useful book

[235] Lucknow 1235 h/1820. The book is extremely rare, since King Ghazi disliked the print and confiscated the whole edition; only a few copies were brought to Europe after the fall of Lucknow 1856. The author died 1840. Cf. ZA X 20, VIII 18.

About the elephant mentioned here, cf. Mrs. Meer Hassan Ali, Observations on the Mussulmauns of India, London 1832, I, 88.

[236] ḥusn al-uswa bimā ṯubita min Allāh wa rasūlihi fī'n-niswa—printed Bhopal 1301 h/1884. About the author cf. Enc. of Islam, s.v., E. G. von Grunebaum–Aziz Ahmad, Muslim Self-Statement in India and Pakistan Wiesbaden 1970.

[237] Woge der Rose, Woge des Weins. Aus dem Urdu und persischen Divan übertragen von A. Schimmel, Zürich 1971. About Ġālib's achievements in Persian: A. C. S. Gilani, Ghalib. His Life and Persian Poetry, Karachi 1962; the most recent edition in 17 vols, Lahore 1969, contains the following Persian works: Prose—dirafš-i kāviānī, Dastanbū, Mihr-i nīmrūz, Panǧ ahang; Poetry — ġazaliyāt-i farsi, qaṣā'id, maṯnawīhā, qiṭ'āt, rubā'īyāt. Cf. S. A. J. Tirmizi, Persian Letters of Ghalib, Delhi 1969. (The literature about Ġālib will be discussed in connection with his Urdu work.)

[238] About him cf. MM 1486.

Haft Asmān 'Seven Heavens' on literary forms,[239] felt obliged to write, in reply to Ġālib's work, a *mu'ayyid-i burhān* 'Supporter of the Argument' in 1865.—Ġālib's account of the Mutiny, *dastanbū* 'Posy of Flowers', is written in such an archaic style, avoiding every Arabic word, that it is difficult to understand. He displays his true strength best in his more than sixty *qaṣīdas*, modelled upon classical poems, among which the religious ones—those directed to God, the Prophet and the twelve imāms—excel by their powerful diction and deep-felt sincerity which is palpable even beneath the thick layer of artistic ornamentation. One should not forget that he even wrote a *maṯnawī* about the finality of Muḥammad's prophethood as a result of his discussions with Maulwī Faḍlulḥaqq, the noted Arabic scholar and theologian of Delhi (d. 1861 in exile in Rangoon).[240]

Ġālib's use of very strange *concetti* renders his Persian sometime difficult even for native speakers of the language. Although he claims to go back to the pure classical idiom, his style, characterized by long chains of infinitives, often in the plural, as well as his whole imagery and choice of words show his close dependence upon the Indian tradition.

In Iqbāl's work, the Persian element is even more prominent than in Ġālib.[241] He, too, has composed the larger part of his work in this language, hoping that his message would reach the Muslims beyond India's borders as well. His style, compared with that of Ġālib whom he deeply admired, is simpler, for his primary interest is to convey a message, not to display literary skill. That is why he prefers memorable and rhythmically strong metres and an imagery which draws heavily upon classical examples; his love for Ǧalāluddīn Rūmī can be clearly seen in his imagery. His message of human freedom, and individual development, of incessant striving in the Goethean sense, his fascinating interpretation of the rôle of Satan in the human process of life prove his indebtedness to the best traditions of Islamic mysticism—however much he attacked the dreaming and revelry of 'pantheistic' mysticism which had beclouded the mind of most Indian Muslims for centuries.[242] He returns, once more, to the roots of Islam, i.e. to the dynamic teachings of the Quran which unfolds, in every moment, new possibilities, and to the classical Sufism which teaches love and suffering for the sake of the highest ideals: his introduction of the figure of Ḥal-

---

239 About him vd. note 42; his qaṣr-i 'irfān, a *taḏkira* of mystics ed. by M. Baqir, Oriental College Magazine, Lahore 1965.

240 ZA III 37, IV 60, VI 71.

241 His Persian works are: asrār-i ḫūdī 'Secrets of the Self' 1915; rumūz-i bēḫūdī 'Mysteries of Selflessness' 1918; payām-i mašriq 'Message of the East,' 1923; zabūr-i 'aǧam 'Persian Psalter' 1927; Ǧāvīdnāme 'Book of Eternity' or 'of Javid,' 1932; Pas či bāyad kard 'What shall now be done,' 1932; Musāfir 'The Traveller' 1934; and parts of Armaġān-i Ḥiǧāz 'Gift of the Higaz,' publ. postumously 1938.

242 Cf. A. Schimmel, Gabriel's Wing. A Study into the religious ideas of Sir Muhammad Iqbal, Leiden 1963 (with an extensive bibliography); Hafeez Malik (ed.), Muhammad Iqbal, Poet-philosopher of Pakistan, New York–London 1971.

lāǧ, the martyr-mystic of Islam, who had been the favourite hero of generations of mystical poets in different languages of the Subcontinent proves that he understood the true character of Islamic religiosity. Ḥallāǧ became, for him, the prototype of the faithful who tried to awaken the slumbering Muslims from the sleep of heedlessness and to call them, once more, into the presence of the Living God—as he has been the hero of those who advocated the sake of love *versus* law, and remained the model even for many contemporary progressive Indo-Muslim writers who endured, like the 10th century mystic, 'gallows and rope' for the sake of freedom. Iqbāl has summed up the best traditions of Indo-Muslim poetry and thought as it had shaped the life of the Subcontinent for almost a millennium.

INDEX